Influential Women

Anne Frank

Other titles in the *Influential Women* series include:

Cleopatra

Hillary Clinton

Malala Yousafzai

Marie Curie

Influential Women

Anne Frank

Peggy J. Parks

ReferencePoint Press®

San Diego, CA

© 2016 ReferencePoint Press, Inc.
Printed in the United States

For more information, contact:
ReferencePoint Press, Inc.
PO Box 27779
San Diego, CA 92198
www. ReferencePointPress.com

LIBRARY OF CONGRESS CATALOGING-IN-PUBLICATION DATA

Parks, Peggy J., 1951- author.
  Anne Frank / by Peggy J. Parks.
     pages cm. -- (Influential women)
  Includes bibliographical references and index.
  ISBN 978-1-60152-946-6 (hardback) -- ISBN 1-60152-946-5 (hardback) 1. Frank, Anne, 1929–1945. 2. Jews--Netherlands--Amsterdam--Biography--Juvenile literature. 3. Jewish children in the Holocaust--Netherlands--Amsterdam--Biography--Juvenile literature. 4. Holocaust, Jewish (1939-1945)--Netherlands--Amsterdam--Juvenile literature. 5. Amsterdam (Netherlands)--Biography--Juvenile literature. I. Title.
  DS135.N6F734986 2016
  940.53'18092--dc23
  [B]
                                                                                2015034208

Contents

Introduction   **6**
  Holding On to Hope

Chapter One   **10**
  Early Childhood in Germany

Chapter Two   **21**
  Evil Closes In

Chapter Three   **32**
  A Secret Existence

Chapter Four   **43**
  The Beginning of the End

Chapter Five   **54**
  A Young Girl's Words Live On

Source Notes   **64**

**Important Events in the
Life of Anne Frank**   **70**

For Further Research   **73**

Index   **75**

Picture Credits   **79**

About the Author   **80**

Introduction

Holding On to Hope

Although it occurred more than seventy years ago, the Holocaust still evokes deep emotional pain and terrifying memories for people throughout the world. From 1941 to 1945, the last four years of World War II, an estimated 6 million Jews were killed by the German Nazi regime—including 1.5 million children. Led by the brutal dictator Adolf Hitler, the Nazis were notoriously anti-Semitic, meaning they despised Jews. "There is no doubt that hatred of Jews constituted the center of Nazi ideology," says historian and Holocaust expert Doris L. Bergen. "Hitler and his associates preached what the scholar Saul Friedländer calls 'redemptive antisemitism': the belief that Jews were the root of all evil and that Germany could be saved from collapse only by total removal of Jews and Jewish influence."[1] In keeping with that anti-Semitic belief, the Nazis set out to rid Germany of its entire Jewish population. Once that had been accomplished, they planned to continue exterminating Jews throughout Europe. This organized execution of millions of Jews was the Holocaust, which remains one of history's most horrific crimes against humanity.

Hundreds of books have been written about the Holocaust, many by noted historians and scholars. But the best-known and most widely read of these was not the work of a scholar or historian; it was written by a young German-born Jewish girl named Anne Frank. For more than two years, Anne recorded her thoughts and dreams in several diaries, the first of which was a present for her thirteenth birthday. The diary, covered in red, tan, and light green plaid cloth, was Anne's most treasured gift. Addressing an imaginary friend she named Kitty, Anne wrote her first entry on June 12, 1942: "I hope I shall be able to confide in you completely as I have never been able to do in anyone before, and I hope that you will be a great support and comfort to me."[2]

Diminishing Freedoms

By the time Anne was four years old, Hitler had come to power in Germany. Her parents, Otto and Edith Frank, knew he despised Jews, which meant they had to leave the country; staying would be much too dangerous. In 1933 the Franks moved to Amsterdam, Holland, in the Netherlands. Anne started school there and became known as a lively girl with a bright, cheery outlook. She was outgoing, friendly, and not afraid to speak her mind.

As the years went by, the Franks could see that their adopted country was not the safe haven they believed it to be. Germany had invaded several European countries, and many Dutch people (especially Jews) feared that the Netherlands would be next—which proved to be correct. In May 1940, with tanks and infantry on the ground and bombers in the air, German forces roared into Holland. The Dutch army fought back but was no match for the Nazis' military strength, and four days later the Dutch government surrendered. The Nazis were now in control of the Netherlands.

> *"There is no doubt that hatred of Jews constituted the center of Nazi ideology."[1]*
>
> —Doris L. Bergen, historian and Holocaust expert.

The life that the Franks had come to know in Amsterdam changed dramatically. "After May 1940 good times rapidly fled," Anne wrote. "First the war, then the capitulation [surrender], followed by the arrival of the Germans, which is when the sufferings of us Jews really began."[3] She explained that the Jews were robbed of most of their rights, from where they were allowed to go to when they were allowed to be outside. But ever the cheerful optimist, Anne tried to find the bright side: "Our freedom was strictly limited. Yet things were still bearable."[4]

In Hiding

It was June 20, 1942, when Anne wrote that life was "still bearable." Less than three weeks later, her world changed more drastically than she ever could have imagined. Otto told Anne and her older sister, Margot, that the family was going into hiding. It was widely known that Jews were being rounded up and taken to concentration camps in Germany and some controlled territories, where their fate could be

Anne Frank started keeping a diary when she was thirteen years old. The words of this young woman who experienced persecution, war, and brutal captivity have touched millions of readers, reminding them of the tragedies that can arise from intolerance and prejudice.

anything from forced labor to death in a gas chamber. Anne's parents were convinced that their only chance of survival was to hide until the Nazis could be overthrown by the Allies. In 1942 Anne, Margot, and their parents moved into a hidden space at the back of a building in

Amsterdam. Before long they were joined by four other Jews who also needed a safe place to hide: Hermann and Auguste van Pels and their teenage son, Peter; and Fritz Pfeffer.

With the help of a few trusted friends on the outside, everyone living in the attic space tried to make the best of a confined, uncomfortable, and frequently unpleasant situation. As the days, weeks, and months dragged on, Anne continued to write in her diary. Even after being in hiding for more than two years, she clung to the steadfast belief that they would all be rescued soon.

Fighting for Life

That was not to be, however. On August 4, 1944, based on an anonymous tip, the Gestapo (German secret police) raided the attic and arrested all eight occupants. They were first taken to a transit camp and then transported to a concentration camp in Nazi-occupied Poland. In November Anne and Margot were transferred to a different camp in northern Germany known as Bergen-Belsen. Once there, the girls became slave laborers.

Bergen-Belsen was severely overcrowded, and conditions were deplorable: scarce food and even scarcer water, no lighting, and lice-infested mattresses. Within a few months of their arrival, Anne and Margot were weak and emaciated from malnutrition, dehydration, and exhaustion. They were both stricken with a deadly disease called typhus and died during the winter of 1945. Less than one month after the girls died, British troops arrived at the camp to set all the surviving prisoners free.

Although Anne did not live to see the liberation she had dreamed of, her diary and journals survived and were published after the war ended. Through her writings people throughout the world have learned about the unspeakable horrors of the Holocaust. They have also gotten to know a remarkable young woman, who symbolizes the power of the human spirit and the ability to carry on even in the face of unspeakable tragedy and heartbreak.

"After May 1940 good times rapidly fled. First the war, then the capitulation [surrender], followed by the arrival of the Germans, which is when the sufferings of us Jews really began."[3]

—Anne Frank, diary entry, June 20, 1942.

Chapter One

Early Childhood in Germany

In the early morning hours of June 12, 1929, Edith (Holländer) Frank delivered a baby girl at a women's clinic in Frankfurt, Germany. The second daughter born to Edith and Otto Frank, the baby was named Annelies Marie, and she became known as Anne. She had trouble breathing at first, which was worrisome. So it was an immense relief when she let out a few strong, robust cries. Unfortunately for her parents, the tiny infant with the powerful lungs continued crying practically nonstop for the next few weeks. Historical author Melissa Müller says that in contrast to Margot, who hardly ever cried as a baby, "Anne's strong will . . . was a challenge, her restlessness exhausting."[5]

As the weeks turned into months, Anne's crying diminished—but her willfulness did not. She frequently tested her mother's patience and demanded a great deal of attention. But she was also an enchanting little girl, as Müller explains: "With her natural charm and liveliness she usually got what she wanted. Everyone—her babysitter, her grandmother, and above all her father—found her impish smile and infectious laughter irresistible. If snuggling close and gazing up with her big eyes failed to do the trick, she cried piteously."[6] Anne's headstrong disposition as a child proved to be indicative of the bold, outspoken young lady she would become in the years ahead.

The City on the River

The city of Anne's birth is often called Frankfurt am Main (pronounced *mine*) because it lies on the banks of the river Main. In the 1920s (as now), Frankfurt was a vibrant, bustling city, one of Germany's major business hubs. In his book *Anne Frank: Silent Witnesses*, author Ronald Wilfred Jansen writes: "Because of its strategic location at the river Main, Frankfurt am Main grew into a major trade centre over the course of the centuries."[7] Frankfurt was home to important institutions such as the Rothschild Bank, which first opened in 1798; and the Frankfurt Stock Exchange, one of the first stock exchanges in the world. One of the largest railway stations in all of Europe was located in Frankfurt, as were the University of Frankfurt and the historic opera house, which was built in 1880.

Frankfurt was founded in 794, and Jews began moving there a few hundred years later. By the early 1800s Frankfurt's Jewish population totaled thirty-three hundred, and by 1871 it had jumped to more than ten thousand. Increasing numbers of Jews continued to move there over the following years. During the 1920s nearly thirty thousand Jews lived in Frankfurt, and it was second only to Berlin, Germany's capital city, in the size of its Jewish population. Frankfurt even had a Jewish mayor, Ludwig Landmann, who was elected in 1924.

> *"Anne's strong will . . . was a challenge, her restlessness exhausting."*[5]
>
> —Melissa Müller, Anne Frank biographer.

Family History

Frankfurt had been home to Otto Frank's family for generations, and he had been born and raised there. His father, Michael Frank, founded a bank in Frankfurt in 1890. He also started a business called Bad Soden Mineral Products, a company that produced throat lozenges. The business was so named because it was located in the town of Bad Soden, which was known for its mineral-rich hot springs. At the time Anne was born, Otto was in charge of the Bad Soden business.

Otto's family was wealthy and influential. As biographer Francine Prose writes: "Otto grew up in a close-knit, assimilated German-Jewish community, surrounded by art and good furniture. Servants. Parties every week."[8] After studying economics at Heidelberg University in Germany, Otto moved to the United States, where he lived and worked in New York City for two years in order to gain business experience. In 1915 he was drafted into the German army and served as a lieutenant during World War I.

Edith had also been born and raised in Germany, but not Frankfurt. She was from the German city of Aachen, which is located about 160 miles (257 km) from Frankfurt, near the borders of Belgium and the Netherlands. Edith's family was also wealthy, and they lived a very comfortable life in Aachen. This was largely due to the success of Edith's father, Abraham Holländer, who was a shrewd businessman. He had built the family's scrap-iron business into a prosperous wholesale metal operation that was one of the leading companies in Aachen. Edith continued to live in her family home until May 1925, when she and Otto were married.

Life in Frankfurt

After their honeymoon in Italy, the newlyweds moved in with Otto's mother, Alice Betty Stern Frank, who had managed the house by herself since her husband's death in 1909. Such arrangements had long been customary for married couples in both the Frank and Holländer families. Alice lived in an area of Frankfurt known as Westend, one of the city's most fashionable neighborhoods, and her home was quite grand. "The large, stately urban villa was suitable for the well-to-do upper middle class," says Jansen. "It was located in an elegant residential area, and had a separate entrance for servants, three balconies at the front, a dome, a central tower, and a large garden."[9]

"Otto [Frank] grew up in a close-knit, assimilated German-Jewish community, surrounded by art and good furniture. Servants. Parties every week."[8]

—Francine Prose, Anne Frank biographer.

Otto and Edith continued living with his mother for two years, and during the first year their daughter Margot was born. When she was a toddler, the Franks decided to break family tradition and move to a place of their own. They rented a spacious home on a quiet street called Marbachweg, which was located on the outskirts of the city. The neighborhood was much less fashionable than where they had previously lived, but the Franks did not care about that. The house had plenty of room, including a guest bedroom for Otto's mother when she came to visit. The area had a rural feel, with plenty of grassy areas for Margot to play.

Shown here is the home at 307 Marbachweg in Frankfurt, where Anne lived as a child.

The Marbachweg neighborhood was far more integrated than where the Franks had previously lived. In Westend about one-fifth of the population was Jewish, compared with Marbachweg, where the Franks were one of the only Jewish families. But, says Müller, "despite different social and religious backgrounds, the adults were friendly and got along well." She adds that the children also got along and played together harmoniously, which was pleasing to the Franks. "They wanted their daughters to grow up without self-consciousness or prejudice," says Müller. "Fortunately, after years of anti-Semitic agitation, the mood in Germany seemed to have calmed down. Right-wing politicians had blamed the Jews for Germany's defeat in World War I and for the economic and social crisis of the early 1920s. But in recent years the economy had begun to improve."[10]

The Downward Slide

Despite signs of economic improvement, many Germans were still bitter about the aftermath of World War I: specifically, the harsh de-

Nazis Strut Their Power

In May 1933, a few months after Adolf Hitler became Germany's chancellor, his minister of propaganda, Joseph Goebbels, organized a massive public book burning. The purpose of this, according to historian and Holocaust expert Doris L. Bergen, was to present "intimidating spectacles of Nazi force." Once the event was announced, thousands of pro-Nazi students were eager to participate. Along with other Nazi supporters, the students made enormous bonfires in which they burned books by Albert Einstein and other noted Jewish authors. They also burned books written by Communists, liberals, and foreigners such as Jack London from the United States. Says Bergen: "Such scenes must have communicated a clear threat to outsiders and critics of Nazism."

In addition to book burnings, Nazis demonstrated their power through pageantry. During the first few months of Hitler's rule, storm troopers marched in innumerable torchlight parades. Often they sang as they marched. Says Bergen: "Supporters adapted old songs and wrote reams of new ones, everything from sentimental folk songs to outright vicious fighting songs, with lyrics about 'Jewish blood' spurting from German knives."

Doris L. Bergen, *The Holocaust: A Concise Encyclopedia.* Lanham, MD: Rowman & Littlefield, 2009, p. 64.

mands on Germany as specified in the Treaty of Versailles. This peace treaty, which formally ended the war, was finalized and signed in June 1919. Because Germany was viewed as the war's chief instigator, the country was hit especially hard by the mandates of the treaty. Germany was required to concede territories to Belgium, Czechoslovakia, and Poland, as well as return the Alsace and Lorraine regions to France. But the demands did not end there, as the US Holocaust Memorial Museum explains: "Perhaps the most humiliating portion of the treaty for the defeated Germany was Article 231, commonly known as the 'War Guilt Clause,' which forced Germany to accept complete responsibility for initiating World War I."[11] By accepting blame for starting the war, Germany became liable for all material damages caused by the war—which totaled billions of dollars in reparation payments.

By the late 1920s, although Germany's economic woes were by no means resolved, the outlook seemed brighter. The Franks were optimistic about this and hoped that the economic upswing would continue. "Edith and Otto felt sufficiently encouraged to hope for greater security," says Müller. "Nineteen twenty-seven was a good year for business in general, and the political parties of the liberal center, which the Franks favored, promised that things would continue to improve."[12] People living in Frankfurt as well as in cities and towns throughout Germany shared the Franks' optimism.

Then on October 24, 1929, when Anne was four months old, a financial catastrophe in the United States crushed the hopes of people throughout the world. The New York Stock Exchange crashed, which in turn caused the collapse of the American economy. Like shock waves from an earthquake, effects of the crash reverberated far beyond America's borders. "As economies were linked together," says the London Jewish Cultural Centre, "the rest of the world suffered too."[13] Once again, Germany was thrown into a state of economic chaos. In addition to its reparation payments, the country owed a great deal of money to the United States. The United States had granted loans to Germany during the 1920s and now wanted them repaid. Germany was unable to comply with that demand.

Banks all over the world were ruined by the stock market crash, with smaller banks especially hard-hit. The Michael Frank Bank, whose specialty was international transactions, lost 90 percent of its business as a direct result of the crash. Müller explains that the Bad Soden company also suffered a financial blow: "People worried about losing their jobs, and the unemployed endured their sore throats and hoarseness without cough drops."[14]

The Nazis Rise to Power

With the German economy in tatters, frustration and anger were rampant. Unemployment was growing at unprecedented rates: By May 1932 the number of Germans who had lost their jobs reached nearly 6 million. With the economy in a downward spiral and no end in sight, people started searching for a scapegoat—and incited by Adolf Hitler, decided Jews should be singled out. "Even though Jews comprised less than one percent of the total German population in 1933 (600,000)," says the Anti-Defamation League, "Hitler used anti-Semitism as a political weapon to gain popular support, blaming Jews for all of Germany's problems. . . . That Hitler's accusations were blatantly contradictory and his facts often fabricated made little difference."[15]

Adolf Hitler and his National Socialist German Workers' Party (better known as the Nazis) were in a perfect position to exploit the growing anger and discontent in Germany. When the party first formed in January 1919, few people were aware of it. As time went by and the Nazi Party became better known, many considered it to be a radical splinter group that had little or no chance of ever attaining political power. In the 1924 elections, the Nazis ran against established parties holding seats in the Reichstag (German parliament) and won just 3 percent of the vote. But by the early 1930s, with the widespread anger and growing mistrust of government, the Germans began to yearn for a new leader. This provided the perfect opportunity for Hitler to step in and tell the people exactly what they wanted to hear. The US Holocaust Memorial Museum writes: "Hitler was a powerful and spellbinding speaker who attracted a wide following of Germans desperate for change. He promised the disenchanted a better life and a new and glorious Germany. The Nazis appealed especially to the unemployed, young people, and members of the lower middle class (small store owners, office employees, craftsmen, and farmers)."[16]

> "Hitler was a powerful and spellbinding speaker who attracted a wide following of Germans desperate for change."[16]
>
> —US Holocaust Memorial Museum.

Hitler's rise to power happened amazingly fast. During the July 1932 elections, the Nazis again challenged the Reichstag—and this time, with more than one-third of the votes, they won enough seats to gain control. The following January Hitler was appointed chancellor, or head of the German government. "Many Germans believed they had found a savior for their nation,"[17] says the US Holocaust Memorial Museum.

Adolf Hitler rose to power as head of a workers' party that pledged to recover the pride of a Germany that had suffered defeat in World War I and economic ruin in the two decades that followed. Part of his platform was to blame the Jews for the nation's misfortunes.

Escalating Fear

Otto and Edith were visiting friends when news of Hitler's chancellorship came on the radio. A second news report covered what was happening in Berlin as a result of Hitler's new power. The newscaster said that a group of Nazi storm troopers were marching through the streets of the city carrying torches and singing anti-Semitic songs about splattering Jewish blood. On the radio the Franks could hear people screaming and cheering in the background—and then their host expressed enthusiasm about what the new leader might be able to do for Germany. Otto later said, "I was speechless, my wife stunned."[18]

Otto had read *Mein Kampf*, Hitler's autobiographical manifesto that was filled with shocking statements about how the German government should have "exterminated the Jews mercilessly" at the beginning of World War I. Hitler further claimed that Germany would not have lost the war if the country had "gassed 12,000 or 15,000"[19] Jews. As

Robbing Jews of Freedom

When Otto and Edith Frank decided to leave Germany with their daughters and immigrate to the Netherlands, they felt that they had no choice. The situation in Frankfurt had become increasingly dangerous for Jews. Since Adolf Hitler had taken control of the German government, the freedoms Jews had long enjoyed—the same freedoms enjoyed by everyone in Germany—were fast disappearing.

On April 1, 1933, less than three months after becoming Germany's dictator, Hitler ordered a national boycott of Jewish-owned retail shops, department stores, and offices of Jewish professionals such as doctors and lawyers. Nazi storm troopers stood menacingly in front of these establishments in order to intimidate people into staying away from them. The US Holocaust Memorial Museum explains: "The Star of David was painted in yellow and black across thousands of doors and windows, with accompanying antisemitic slogans. Signs were posted saying 'Don't Buy from Jews' and 'The Jews Are Our Misfortune.' Throughout Germany, acts of violence against individual Jews and Jewish property occurred; the police intervened only rarely."

Although this national boycott lasted only a day and was ignored by many Germans, it was a forewarning of what was to come: a nationwide crusade by the Nazi Party to destroy the entire Jewish population in Germany.

US Holocaust Memorial Museum, "Boycott of Jewish Businesses," June 20, 2014. www.ushmm.org.

horrifying as this was to Otto when he read the book, he dismissed it as the hysterical ranting of a madman. He always believed that Hitler was far too radical to achieve any position of power. But now, Otto had to face the truth. This man, whose main objective was ridding Germany of its entire Jewish population, was in a position to accomplish that.

In March 1933, two months after Hitler was appointed chancellor, the newly elected parliament passed the Enabling Act. This law effectively ended democracy in Germany and established Hitler as the legal dictator. Within days Jews became the target of increasing hatred and bigotry. Doris L. Bergen writes: "Hitler's Nazis used a combination of intimidation and legislation to create a mood of hostility toward Germany's Jews, a kind of open season for abuse."[20] Jewish businesses were boycotted, and potential customers were frightened away by storm troopers. Nazis staged public humiliation of Jews and friends of Jews. Schools did nothing to stop Jewish children from being bullied—and even sanctioned it. Then, one by one Jews' civil rights were taken away.

Fearing for the lives of seven-year-old Margot and four-year-old Anne, as well as their own lives, the Franks reluctantly decided to leave

A photo of Anne and her older sister, Margot. When Margot was seven and Anne was four, Otto and Edith Frank decided to leave Germany. The Nazi Party was inciting discrimination and violence against German Jews, so the Franks moved west to the Netherlands.

Germany. They chose to move to the Netherlands, where Otto had a business opportunity in the capital city of Amsterdam. Moving there appealed to Otto for a number of reasons. For one, the Dutch people were known for being liberal and tolerant; Jews, who made up 10 percent of Amsterdam's population, were thoroughly integrated and accepted. Another plus was that Otto spoke Dutch and was familiar with the city of Amsterdam. Together he and Edith agreed that this was where they would start a new life.

In midsummer 1933 Otto moved to Amsterdam to set up his new business and prepare for his wife and daughters to join him. By June 1934 the family members were settled in their new home, where they felt safe for the first time in a long time. Years later, in a letter to a friend, Otto reflected on his decision to leave Germany. He was sickened by what he saw happening to so many of his countrymen, watching them "turning into hordes of nationalistic, cruel, antisemitic criminals." Otto went on to say: "I had to face the consequences, and though this did hurt me deeply, I realized that Germany was not the world and I left my country forever."[21]

> "Though this did hurt me deeply, I realized that Germany was not the world and I left my country forever."[21]
>
> —Otto Frank, Anne Frank's father.

Chapter Two

Evil Closes In

It was June 12, 1934, and Anne Frank was giddy with excitement. It was her fifth birthday, and some of her friends were coming over later for a party. Celebrating birthdays every year with a festive party was a family tradition the Franks had brought with them from Frankfurt. Both Anne and Margot loved the yearly custom.

That afternoon several little girls with whom Anne had made friends arrived with presents for her. They enjoyed refreshments, and each girl received a party favor such as a tea set for her dolls. Being a child who thrived on attention, Anne was in her element as the birthday girl—the star of the day. "Anne was the perfect hostess," says Melissa Müller. "She swept others along with her enthusiasm and her infectious giggling. Her lively prattle was still mostly in German, but Dutch words had begun to crop up in her speech."[22]

New School, New Friends

Aside from a few weeks of missing her friends back in Frankfurt, Anne had adjusted well to her new life in Amsterdam. But she was impatient to attend school like her big sister and teased her mother relentlessly to let her go. Finally, there was a kindergarten opening at the Montessori school. Otto and Edith thought this type of school, which emphasized self-motivation, individuality, and developing children's natural interests, would be a good fit for Anne.

When the day arrived for Anne to start kindergarten, her mother was concerned that she might be scared. Yet Edith need not have worried. With Anne's outgoing, bubbly personality, she began making friends right away. She was especially excited when Hanneli (also called Hanne) Goslar entered the classroom. The girls had first seen each other a few days before at a grocery store when their mothers struck up a conversation in German. The women discovered that both their families had emigrated from Germany and also that they lived next door to each other. As they were chatting, their daughters peered at one another with curiosity and interest.

Soon after Edith walked Anne to school and dropped her off at her classroom, Hanneli arrived. Right away she noticed Anne across the room. "She was making music on little bells," says Hanneli. "I didn't know anyone. I didn't know the language. I wanted to go home." She changed her mind as soon as Anne saw her, as she explains: "She turned around and ran into my arms. From that moment we were friends, and then our parents made friends through us."[23]

Anne loved school and was well liked by her classmates, both boys and girls. She was not at all shy; in fact, she adored being the center of attraction. "Her cheerfulness, inventiveness, and love of mischief made her popular," says Müller. "She showed her domineering and possessive side only when she didn't get her way."[24] Along with Hanneli, Anne also became close friends with another little girl named Susanne (also called Sanne) Ledermann. The three of them were soon inseparable and became known as Anne, Hanne, and Sanne.

> "Amsterdam always had a tradition of sheltering people who had run from tyranny of one sort or another."[25]
>
> —Miep Gies, Otto Frank's secretary.

The Joy of Feeling Free

The Franks were among thousands of Jewish immigrants who had fled Germany for the Netherlands after Hitler assumed power. Many of these people settled in Amsterdam. Although the city was not exclusively Jewish, it was home to a large Jewish population. By the end of the 1930s, Amsterdam was home to an estimated ten thousand Jews who had left their native countries behind. "Amsterdam always had a tradition of sheltering people who had run from tyranny of one sort or another,"[25] says Miep Gies, an Austrian-born woman who was Otto Frank's secretary and a close friend of the family.

The Franks had moved to a street called Merwedeplein, which was in South Amsterdam's river district. Their apartment was in one of the

Suffering humiliation and sometimes injury, German Jews fled their homeland in search of security in other lands. Some closed down their businesses and sold their homes; others fled with what possessions they could carry as anti-Jewish persecution became law under the Nazis.

many red brick homes that line the canals. Merwedeplein formed a triangular-shaped plaza with a grassy area that was separated from the street by bushes and trees. This was an ideal place for children to play, as Müller explains:

> In the trees and shrubbery and on the grass in the middle of the plaza, the children played hide-and-seek, tag, and catch, and shot marbles. There were always enough children for games like stickball. The girls did handstands and cartwheels and jumped rope. On the sidewalks they played hopscotch, raced about on scooters and roller skates, and rolled hoops, whipping them along with small sticks.[26]

After being threatened and fearful in Germany, Otto and Edith were relieved to have left that behind. They felt safe in the Netherlands. It had not been easy for them to leave their native Germany; especially for Edith, who missed her former home and family very much. But she and Otto knew they were much better off in Amsterdam. They were confident that their decision to relocate was the right one for their daughters and for themselves. Anne grew accustomed to her new surroundings quickly—and as always, she loved being the center of attention. In school, says Goslar, Anne sat in the front of the class "so that she could do funny things." Goslar recalls one particular stunt for which Anne became known. "She could do this trick where she could take her shoulder out of its socket. You couldn't see it but you could hear her making this 'knock, knock, knock' sound. That made everyone laugh, which made Anne very happy. She liked the attention."[27]

Gies also observed Anne's penchant for making people laugh and says this came naturally because she was funny. "Anne had developed the skill of mimicry," says Gies. "She would mimic anyone and anything, and very well at that: the cat's meow, her friend's voice, her teacher's authoritative tone. We couldn't help laughing at her little performance, she was so skilled with her voice. Anne loved having an attentive audience, and loved to hear us respond to her skits and clowning."[28]

The Franks' home was a popular gathering place for the neighborhood children. Anne's parents emphasized that the girls' friends were always welcome there. One attraction was the delicious food, because Edith was a superb cook. "Mrs. Frank served delicious rolls topped with cream cheese and chocolate bits, cold lemonade, and bottled milk, a particular treat,"[29] says Müller.

Over the next several years, the Franks settled into normal family life in Amsterdam. Anne and Margot liked school and enjoyed being with their friends. They played games and read books. The family took vacations at the seashore and captured the memories with dozens of photographs. The Franks' home was filled with friends, fun, laughter, and good food. Finally, life seemed to be treating them well, and they were happy. But in the autumn of 1938, the Franks' sense of peace and well-being began to unravel. They were forced to acknowledge that their safe haven was not so safe after all.

The Nuremberg Race Laws

In mid-September 1935, during the annual party rally in Nuremberg, Germany, Nazi officials presented two anti-Jewish laws that took effect immediately. The first, called the Law for the Protection of German Blood and German Honor, prohibited Jews from marrying or having sexual relations with people of German or related heritage (Aryans). The Reich Citizenship Law distinguished between "Reich citizens" and "subjects," thereby stripping Jews of their German citizenship. Additional laws soon followed that further deprived Jews of their rights.

An unintended consequence of these laws was widespread confusion over the Nazis' failure to define a Jew. So they distributed charts that described Jews as anyone who had three or four Jewish grandparents. This definition applied "regardless of whether that individual identified himself or herself as a Jew or belonged to the Jewish religious community," says the US Holocaust Memorial Museum. "Many Germans who had not practiced Judaism for years found themselves caught in the grip of Nazi terror. Even people with Jewish grandparents who had converted to Christianity were defined as Jews." Along with descriptive text, the charts included illustrations that showed Jews as black figures, Germans of mixed race as shaded figures, and Aryans as white figures.

US Holocaust Memorial Museum, "The Nuremberg Race Laws." www.ushmm.org.

Growing Danger

News reports from Germany told of how the Nazis were becoming more vicious and unpredictable. Otto and Edith learned of violent anti-Jewish uprisings known as "pogroms" that were sanctioned by the Nazi regime. *Pogrom* is a Russian word that means "to wreak havoc; to demolish violently"—a fitting description of what occurred in early November 1938. Gangs of Nazis carried out an unprecedented wave of violence and destruction in German cities and towns. "Hundreds of

Jewish businesses, shops, and homes had been smashed and burned in Germany," says Gies. "Jewish synagogues had been destroyed, along with Jewish holy books, and thousands of Jewish people had been beaten or shot. . . . In an inferno of broken glass and destruction, thousands of Jews had been gathered up and deported to parts unknown."[30] The November 1938 pogrom came to be known as *Kristallnacht*, which is German for "night of broken glass."

The threat posed by the Nazi regime was no longer confined to Germany. The Germans had annexed Austria in March 1938, and within a year their armies had invaded Poland and Czechoslovakia. Denmark and Norway fell to attack in April 1940. Fear was growing among the Dutch people that the Netherlands would be next, but many refused to believe it. The country had maintained a policy of neutrality during World War I, as Webster University professor Linda M. Woolf writes: "While many of their neighbors fell to the Germans during World War I, the Netherlands remained outside of the war. With the advent of World War II, the Netherlands sought to again remain neutral." Hitler himself had issued a statement vowing to respect the country's neutrality. But, says Woolf, "as with so many other promises made by Hitler and the Nazis, this assurance proved worthless."[31] On May 10, 1940, less than eight months after Hitler's statement, the Germans invaded Holland.

The Dreaded Invasion

The Dutch army fought a valiant fight, but its soldiers were no match for the heavily armed, powerful German military. German planes bombed the city of Rotterdam, and the Nazis warned of dire consequences if a full surrender did not occur promptly. On the evening of May 14, four days after the invasion began, the Netherlands military commander came on the radio with an announcement. He explained, says Gies, "that the Germans had obliterated Rotterdam with bombs dropped from the air; that floods were spreading across sections of Holland through opened dikes; that the Germans had threatened to bomb Utrecht and Amsterdam if we continued to resist. In order to spare further loss of life and property . . . we were surrendering to the Germans."[32] The brutal attack was over. The Netherlands was now under the control of the Germans.

Surprisingly, the Nazis behaved differently from what the Dutch people had expected. After invading Poland and Czechoslovakia, the Nazis immediately passed restrictive anti-Jewish legislation, but that did not happen in the Netherlands. Francine Prose explains: "The good times lasted slightly longer in the Netherlands than they did in other Nazi-occupied countries, in part because the invaders wished to preserve good relations with the Dutch, fellow Aryans whom they hoped might welcome the chance to join an ethnically pure greater Germany." Prose adds, however, that "despite the gradual pace at which the Nazis implemented anti-Jewish regulations in Holland, their intentions soon became clear."[33]

> "Despite the gradual pace at which the Nazis implemented anti-Jewish regulations in Holland, their intentions soon became clear."[33]
>
> —Francine Prose, Anne Frank biographer.

Freedom Stripped Away

Beginning in midsummer 1940, the Jews' rights were steadily taken away. They were not allowed to work in university or government jobs, and those who did were fired. Jewish newspapers were shut down. Jews were prohibited from driving cars or riding streetcars. They were forced to turn in their bicycles even though cycling was the main form of transportation in Amsterdam. There were numerous other anti-Jewish rules, as Anne wrote on June 20, 1942:

> Jews are only allowed to do their shopping between three and five o'clock and then only in shops which bear the placard "Jewish shop." Jews must be indoors by eight o'clock and cannot even sit in their own gardens after that hour. Jews are forbidden to visit theatres, cinemas, and other places of entertainment. Jews may not take part in public sports. Swimming baths, tennis courts, hockey fields, and other sports grounds are all prohibited to them.[34]

To distinguish Jews from all others, the Nazis ordered yellow six-pointed cloth stars to be sewn on clothing of Jewish men, women, and children. *Jew* was printed in black letters on the cloth star. (In Neth-

To identify Jews among the larger population, the Nazis required all Jews to register with local authorities and to wear a Star of David on their clothing. The sewn-on patch made it easy for Nazis and their sympathizers to harass Jews on the streets.

erlands, this was written as *JOOD*; in Germany, as *Jude*; in France, as *Juif.*) "The star was to be firmly stitched to outer garments, such as overcoats, suit coats, and dresses," says Müller, "and not just anywhere but breast-high on the left side and fully visible."[35] Jews were forbidden from going outside without the star.

Also, the Nazis forbade Jews from having any association whatsoever with Christians. One result of this was that Jewish children had to leave their current schools and attend schools for Jews only. It was hard for Anne to leave the Montessori school and one of her favorite teachers, Mrs. Kuperus. As she explained: "I had to say good-by to Mrs. K. We both wept, it was very sad."[36] But Anne became accustomed to her new school, the Jewish Lyceum, and before too long was happy there. She was a popular girl and, true to her nature, was known for being funny.

Even as their rights were being stripped away by the Nazis, Otto and Edith did their best to keep family life as normal as possible. They tried to make their daughters feel secure and happy, but that was becoming more difficult by the day. The truth was, they lived in constant uncertainty about what might befall them with Hitler in power. "Fear and anxiety dominated everyday life," says Müller. "For some time, there had been rumors that Jews were being picked up, with or without warning, in their homes or on the street. . . . In late June 1942 word spread that the Germans were planning to systematically deport all the Jews living in Holland. Nobody knew where

Mature Beyond Her Years

From the time she was a little girl, Anne Frank was outgoing and unafraid to speak her mind. "She spoke candidly about all kinds of things," says Miep Gies, who was secretary to Otto Frank and a friend of the family. "She was aware of everything going on in the outside world. She was very indignant about the injustices being heaped on the Jewish people."

Because of her close relationship with the Franks, Gies watched Anne mature from a little girl to a lovely teenager. She writes: "In addition to all Anne's many interests, like famous film stars and her best girlfriends, a new subject had gotten her attention: boys. Her talk now was spiced with chatter about particular young people of the opposite sex." Yet as normal as these changes were, Gies was saddened that Anne seemed to be growing up too fast. "It was as though the terrible events in the outside world were speeding up this little girl's development," says Gies, "as though Anne were suddenly in a hurry to know and experience everything. On the outside, Anne was a delicate, vivacious not-quite-twelve-year-old girl, but on the inside, a part of her was suddenly much older."

Miep Gies with Alison Leslie Gold, *Anne Frank Remembered*. New York: Glencoe/McGraw-Hill, 2002, p. 43.

they were to be sent or for what purpose. To Germany or somewhere else? To Poland, as the BBC had reported? The only certain thing was that no one was safe."[37]

Otto and Edith considered all possibilities. They checked into immigrating to the United States, but red tape and enormous backlogs kept them from doing so. Finally, the Franks decided their only option was to hide for an indefinite period of time. They chose the building that housed Otto's business, which faced the Prinsengracht canal. Above the back of the building was an extension that could not be seen from the front because of the buildings that surrounded it. The extension had two stories and an attic, and it was large enough for all of them. Gies agreed without hesitation to help—even though she was risking severe punishment or death by doing so. Several others agreed to help as well, including Gies's husband, Jan; and three of Otto's employees: Victor Kugler, Johannes Kleiman, and Bep Voskuijl.

During early July 1942 the Franks told Anne and Margot about their plans. Otto explained that for several months, Gies, her husband, Kugler, and Kleiman had been moving food and supplies into the secret location little by little. Anne was taken aback by this news. "But Daddy, when would it be?" she asked. Otto told Anne not to worry, that everything was being taken care of, and to enjoy her carefree life while she still could. "That was all," she said. "Oh, may the fulfillment of those somber words remain far distant yet!"[38] When Anne wrote that diary entry, she had no way of knowing that the "distant" time she was hoping for was less than twenty-four hours away.

Time to Go

On Sunday, July 5, 1942, Anne was outside on the veranda reading a book. The postman arrived with a registered letter for Margot: an official summons known as a "call-up." This was her directive to report to a Nazi work camp in Germany along with thousands of other Jews. "I was stunned," Anne wrote. "A call-up, everyone knows what that

Fearing for the safety of his family in occupied Amsterdam, Otto Frank had a few rooms at the rear part of his business sealed off to form a secret living space. This hidden annex was only accessible through a door shielded in the daytime by a bookcase.

means. Visions of concentration camps and lonely cells raced through my head."[39]

Otto and Edith had no intention of turning their sixteen-year-old daughter over to the Nazis. Their plans had been made. Their secret place was ready. It was time for the Franks to go into hiding, and they would leave early the next morning.

Chapter Three

A Secret Existence

"We only wanted to get away, only escape and arrive safely, nothing else."[40] Anne Frank's chilling words convey the desperation she and her family felt as they walked from home to their hiding place. Yet they had to act like nothing was out of the ordinary—their lives depended on it. They could not hurry, lest they draw attention to themselves. They could not carry bags of their possessions. All the clothes they took had to be worn, as Anne explained: "No Jew in our situation would have dreamed of going out with a suitcase full of clothing." By the time she had finished putting on everything she wanted to take, Anne could barely move. "I had on two vests, three pairs of pants, a dress, on top of that a skirt, jacket, summer coat, two pairs of stockings, lace-up shoes, woolly cap, scarf, and still more."[41]

Margot had gone ahead with Miep Gies, followed by Anne and her parents about fifteen minutes later. Anne felt like they were heading into the unknown because she had no idea where they were going. "Only when we were on the road did Mummy and Daddy begin to tell me bits and pieces about the plan." Along the way, people driving to work glanced sympathetically at the Franks walking in the pouring rain. "You could see by their faces how sorry they were they couldn't offer us a lift," said Anne. "The gaudy yellow star spoke for itself."[42]

The Secret Annex

When the Franks arrived at the Prinsengracht building, Gies met them at the door. They climbed a wooden staircase to a small landing and entered a door on the right-hand side. This led to the space that Anne called the secret annex. "No one would ever guess that there would be so many rooms hidden behind that plain gray door,"[43] she said. Immediately in front of the doorway was a steep, narrow stairway that led to the second level. To the left of the stairs, Anne later explained to her imaginary diary friend Kitty, "a tiny passage brings you into a room which was to become the Frank family's bed-sitting-room, next door a smaller room, study and bedroom for the two young ladies of the family."[44] On that same floor was a small bathroom that everyone would share.

Up the stairs to the second level was the annex's most spacious room. Anne was surprised at how large and airy it was. "If you open the door," she said, "you are simply amazed that there could be such a big, light room in such an old house by the canal."[45] The room had previously served as a pharmacist's laboratory, so it was equipped with a gas stove, a sink, and cupboards. During the day this large space would serve as a kitchen, dining room, and common living area for everyone. At night it would serve as the bedroom for Hermann and Auguste van Pels and their son, Peter, who would be joining the Franks in a few weeks. Off that room was a small corridor room where Peter would sleep. A stairway in his room led to a large attic with a skylight that could be opened to let in fresh air.

Once the Franks had settled in and had their living space organized, Anne reflected on what it felt like to run away from their home and "disappear," as she described it. "Well," she wrote on July 11, 1942, "all I can say is that I don't know myself yet. I don't think I shall ever feel really at home in this house, but that does not mean I loathe it here; it is more like being on vacation in a very peculiar boarding house. Rather a mad idea, perhaps, but that is how it strikes me."[46] One aspect of their hiding place that Anne loved was hearing the bells ringing in the historic Westerkerk church tower. The church was just across the back gardens from the annex, so the bells were extraordinarily loud. Every fifteen minutes, throughout the day and night, the carillon with its thirty-seven bells played a melody. Anne's parents and Margot could not get used to the sound, but Anne felt differently. "I loved it from the start," she said, "and especially in the night it's like a faithful friend."[47]

> "I don't think I shall ever feel really at home in this house, but that does not mean I loathe it here."[46]
>
> —Anne Frank, diary entry of July 11, 1942.

Nights were the hardest time for Anne because that was when fear and loneliness crept in. "It is the silence that frightens me so in the

The Westerkerk Church was very close to the hidden annex where the Franks lived. Anne recounted in her journal that the chimes from the church's bell tower were a daily comfort. The rest of the hidden group, however, did not share her fondness for the loud ringing.

evenings and at night," she said. "I wish like anything that one of our protectors could sleep here at night. I can't tell you how oppressive it is *never* to be able to go outdoors, also I'm very afraid that we shall be discovered and be shot. That is not exactly a pleasant prospect."[48] Anne was somewhat cheered by knowing that the Van Pels family would soon be moving in. Perhaps then it would not be so quiet.

Three More Fugitives

On Monday, July 13, the Van Pels family arrived. They moved in sooner than planned because of an escalation in violent anti-Jewish uprisings. Surprise attacks known as razzias were on the rise in Amsterdam, with Jews being dragged from their homes, loaded into trucks, and taken away. "The new rash of razzias was raging all across Amsterdam," says Gies. She noticed a stark contrast between the Franks' sad arrival at the annex and that of the Van Pelses, who were "overjoyed to be safely ensconced in their cozy hiding place." Gies writes: "They had much to tell the Franks about what nightmares had been taking place in Amsterdam; so much had happened to their Jewish friends in only one week since the Franks had disappeared."[49]

The Franks were shocked and sickened to hear about what was happening to Jews, many of whom they knew. "Anne, Margot, and Mrs. Frank went gray as they listened," says Gies. "Some of the Jews sitting side by side on these transports had been their own friends and neighbors. Whole streetcars were now filled with Jews wearing yellow stars and carrying allotted bits of luggage."[50] Hearing about the terrible fate of their fellow Jews reinforced the need to take every possible precaution while living in the annex. *Never* was being careful more important than it was now. This included being stringent about following a daily routine because every move they made revolved around the clock.

> *"Whole streetcars were now filled with Jews wearing yellow stars and carrying allotted bits of luggage."*[50]
>
> —Miep Gies, Otto Frank's secretary.

Day-to-Day Living

Other than Otto's four most trusted employees, the workers downstairs knew nothing about the people hiding upstairs. On weekdays the workers arrived at 8:30 a.m., so everyone in the annex had to be up by 7:00 a.m. "Only strict adherence to this rule," says Melissa Müller, "ensured that by eight-thirty they would all have completed their morning toilet, dressed, and stowed their bedding to give them as much living space as the little rooms could provide."[51]

The morning hours were spent on quiet activities: schoolwork, reading, or writing for Anne, Margot, and Peter; reading, sewing,

Who Was the Betrayer?

On the morning of August 4, 1944, the telephone rang at Gestapo headquarters in Amsterdam. The officer in charge, Julius Deetman, answered and was told there were Jews hiding in an annex behind the 263 Prinsengracht building. Whether the caller gave a name is not known. After the war ended, Deetman committed suicide so investigators never questioned him. A police report only confirmed that someone had been paid sixty guilders (about sixty American dollars) for providing the lead.

To this day no one knows who the betrayer was, but there were a few suspects. One was Willem G. van Maaren, the Prinsengracht building's warehouse foreman. The helpers who protected the eight Jews in hiding noticed that Van Maaren often acted suspiciously. He commented about the large amounts of bread and milk that were delivered to the building. He remarked about pencils on Otto Frank's desk that were not there the previous day. He found Hermann van Pels's wallet in Otto's office after it dropped out of Van Pels's coat the night before. And he commented that office workers seemed to be "sneaking around." But still, no proof was ever found that connected Van Maaren to the betrayal. In her biography of Anne Frank, Francine Prose says that Otto himself suspected Van Maaren but chose not to pursue it. She writes: "How would it have helped Otto Frank, or his wife and children, or their Dutch helpers to know who had sold eight lives in exchange for the bounty that the Nazis paid for the fugitive Jews?"

Francine Prose, *Anne Frank: The Book, the Life, the Afterlife*. New York: Harper Perennial, 2010, pp. 52–53.

or paperwork for the adults. At some point during the early morning, Gies crept up the stairs to pick up a shopping list of groceries, personal articles, and other necessities. Even though she could only stay a few minutes, these early morning visits were precious to everyone in the annex. Anne especially perked up because she was so hungry for news from the outside world. "Before she could start her barrage of questions," says Gies, "I'd promise Anne that I'd be back later with the shopping and at that time I'd sit and we could have a real talk."[52]

Each day at 12:30 p.m., the ringing of the Westerkerk bells signaled the start of ninety glorious minutes of freedom for everyone in the annex. Even those who found the bells annoying welcomed them at lunchtime. "The whole mixed crowd breathes again," said Anne. "The warehouse boys have gone home now."[53] For the next hour and a half, they had lunch, listened to the radio, peeled potatoes or shelled peas for dinner, and visited with Gies or others who came to see them one by one. Afternoons were spent much like the mornings, with reading, writing, studying, and whispered conversations. Then it was nap time, which Anne called "the most peaceful hour; everyone is asleep, no one is disturbed."[54]

The tolling of the Westerkerk bells at 5:30 p.m. was an especially welcome sound because it meant the warehouse workers were leaving for the day. Gies or one of the other helpers went to give everyone in the annex the all-clear. "Each one of our friends greeted us happily as we made our way upstairs," says Gies. "'The last worker has gone,' I informed them. Right away, there were voices, footsteps, the toilet flushing, a cabinet shutting. Already, it was noisy upstairs; the place had come alive."[55] The rooms were tidied, dinner was prepared, and conversations took place—often leading to heated debate.

This was also the one time when they could venture out of the annex and down the stairs to Otto's office. There they pulled up chairs and gathered around the table to listen to the evening broadcast on the radio. In blatant violation of Nazi law, the radio was tuned to a British station that broadcast programs by the Dutch resistance movement. "The whole room bristled with excitement," says Gies, "when the near-and-yet-so-far voice of Radio Orange came through the radio . . . filling us with hope and with information, our only real connection to the still-free outside world."[56]

Challenging Times

Throughout the rest of the summer and fall, life remained essentially the same for the people hiding in the annex. There was one notable change, though. On November 16, 1942, Gies's dentist, Fritz Pfeffer, moved in, bringing the total annex residents to eight. Anne was

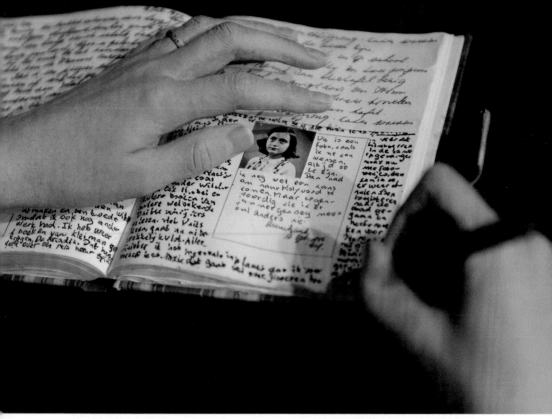

During the long days in the annex, Anne and her sister received lessons in writing and other school subjects. In her free time, Anne continued to practice her writing by filling page after page of her diaries with her thoughts about her family, the war, and growing up.

enthusiastic about having Pfeffer join them, but downhearted to hear the news he had brought. "Countless friends and acquaintances have gone to a terrible fate," she wrote. "Evening after evening the green and gray army lorries [trucks] trundle past. The Germans ring at every front door to inquire if there are any Jews living in the house. If there are, then the whole family has to go at once. . . . It seems like the slave hunts of olden times."[57]

While living in the annex, Anne often reminded herself of how fortunate she and the others were to have a safe place to hide. Sometimes she felt guilty about having food to eat and a warm bed to sleep in while so many other Jews had been captured by the Nazis. She wrote: "I get frightened when I think of close friends who have now been delivered into the hands of the crudest brutes that walk the earth. And all because they are Jews!" Yet Anne and the others could not dwell on the troubling news from outside—their sanity depended on it. "It won't do us any good, or help those outside, to go on being as gloomy as we are at the moment," she said. "And what would be the object of making our 'Secret Annexe' into a 'Secret Annexe of Gloom'? . . . If I want to laugh about something, should I stop myself quickly and feel ashamed that I am cheerful?"[58] No, she decided, there was no point whatsoever in denying herself cheer.

Yet as the days turned into months, it was hard to remain cheerful. As spacious as the annex was, eight people were squeezed into a combined living space of about 530 square feet (50 sq m). In such close quarters conflicts were inevitable—and as time went by, they were cropping up with increasing regularity. In September 1943 Anne wrote: "Relations between us here are getting worse all the time. At mealtimes, no one dares to open their mouths (except to allow a mouthful of food to slip in) because whatever is said you either annoy someone or it is misunderstood."[59]

One of the biggest frustrations for Anne was that Mrs. Van Pels continuously made derogatory comments about her. She called Anne spoiled and said she obviously had not been raised properly. "These are always her first and last words, 'if Anne were my daughter,'" Anne wrote. "Thank heavens I'm not!"[60] Yet Anne was also hyperemotional, because she was an adolescent girl going through the normal hormonal changes of growing up. She was having a great deal of trouble getting along with her mother, did not always like her sister, and had a prickly relationship with Pfeffer. Quite often Anne felt like everyone was against her and was frustrated that she could not let her anger out. She explained:

I'm boiling with rage, and yet I mustn't show it. I'd like to stamp my feet, scream, give Mummy a good shaking, cry, and I don't know what else, because of the horrible words, mocking looks, and accusations which are leveled at me repeatedly every day. . . . If I talk everyone thinks I'm showing off, when I'm silent they think I'm ridiculous; rude if I answer, sly if I get a good idea, lazy if I'm tired, selfish if I eat a mouthful more than I should, stupid, cowardly, crafty, etc. etc. The whole day long I hear nothing else but that I am an insufferable baby, and although I laugh about it and pretend not to take any notice, I *do* mind.[61]

At some point after such emotional times, Anne usually realized that things were not as bad as she had imagined. Also, during her most contemplative moments, she remembered that everyone else was suffering too. "One day we laugh and see the funny side of the situation, but the next we are afraid, fear, suspense, and despair staring from our faces," she wrote in late May 1944. "We've been here for two years now; how long have we still to put up with this almost unbearable,

Fierce Protector, Loyal Friend

For her role in hiding the eight people in the annex, Miep Gies put herself in grave danger. Helping Jews was a crime punishable by imprisonment or death, and Gies knew this. But it did not stop her; she was determined to do whatever she could for them, and she helped them for two years. So when her dear friends were arrested and taken away, she was heartbroken—and determined to fight for them, again putting herself at risk.

The day after the arrest, Gies went to Gestapo headquarters. She offered the arresting officer money if he would free the eight Jews, but he said he could not help her. When she insisted, he told her to go upstairs and see his boss. Trying to remain calm and stop her knees from shaking, Gies climbed the stairs to where high-ranking Nazis were in a meeting. They turned to stare at her, and she asked who was in charge. One got up from his chair, called her an insulting name, pushed her out the door, and slammed the door in her face. Suddenly it occurred to Gies how much danger she could be in. With her heart thudding, she walked toward the door to the building. "Gestapo were everywhere in the corridors," she says, "like flies in fancy uniforms. Again the thought rang in my brain, People who enter this building do not always come out again." She kept walking and was relieved to make it out the door safely. But it was hard to feel happy about her escape when she could not save her friends.

Miep Gies with Alison Leslie Gold, *Anne Frank Remembered*. New York: Glencoe/McGraw-Hill, 2002, p. 147.

Special German police squads roamed neighborhoods, knocking on doors and searching for Jews in hiding. Whether turned in by an informant or simply uncovered by the police units, these Jews were either executed or sent to concentration camps where a horrible life, and probable death, awaited.

ever increasing pressure?"[62] The terrible answer to that question was revealed less than three months later.

The Unthinkable Happens

Friday, August 4, 1944, was a gorgeous summer day in Amsterdam. Inside the secret annex, the Franks, the Van Pelses, and Pfeffer had gone through their usual morning routine. Gies had been upstairs earlier to get the day's grocery list; as usual, Anne was eager to hear the latest news and urged her to stay. "I promised that I'd come back and sit and we could have a real talk in the afternoon when I returned with the groceries," says Gies. "But conversation would have to wait until then."[63] She returned to her office to get started on her work.

Sometime later that morning, for no particular reason, Gies happened to glance up—and saw that she was staring at the barrel of a pistol. She froze. "Stay put," the man ordered. "Don't move."[64] He then went to find the person in charge (Victor Kugler) and demanded to be taken upstairs. There had been an anonymous phone call. The man knew about the secret annex and about the Jews hiding in it. After two years, the day they all hoped and prayed would never come was here. Someone had betrayed them, and the Gestapo was here to take them away.

Chapter Four

The Beginning of the End

After the German police truck sped away with her friends inside, Miep Gies was left stunned and shaken. It did not seem possible that they were gone. She and the other protectors had worked so hard to keep the eight people hidden and safe, but in the end they could not save them. With a heavy heart, she climbed the steps to the annex and unlocked the door. Her immediate impression was disgust at the chaotic mess the officers had left behind. In their quest for whatever valuables they could find, the men had ransacked all the rooms, overturning furniture, pulling drawers out, and emptying their contents onto the floor. The annex, always so neat and tidy when the Franks, Van Pelses, and Pfeffer lived there, was now in shambles.

Gies walked into Otto and Edith's bedroom and saw that the floor was covered with loose sheets of paper—and then another object caught her eye. "On the floor, amidst the chaos of papers and books, my eye lit on the little red-orange checkered, cloth-bound diary that Anne had received for her thirteenth birthday," says Gies. "I remembered how happy Anne had been to receive this little book to write her private thoughts in. I knew how precious her diary was to Anne."[65] Gies picked up the cherished diary and several notebooks that Anne had used for writing when her diary was full. Then she and Bep Voskuijl gathered up all the loose sheets of paper. When they finished, Gies locked the door to the secret annex, and they returned to the office. After only a moment's hesitation, she opened the bottom drawer of her desk and carefully piled the diary, notebooks, and loose papers inside. "I will keep everything," she said. "I'll keep everything safe for Anne until she comes back."[66]

A Deceptive Sense of Being Free

Meanwhile, the Franks, the Van Pelses, and Pfeffer were taken to Gestapo headquarters in South Amsterdam. The men were interrogated regarding the whereabouts of other Jews in hiding. But unlike typical Gestapo interrogations, which dragged on for hours and often involved torture, these sessions were brief. Referring to Otto Frank, Francine Prose writes: "He insisted that, after twenty-five months in the annex, he had no contact with anyone who might be in a situation like his—a claim so clearly logical that even the police were persuaded."[67]

> "I remembered how happy Anne had been to receive this little book to write her private thoughts in. I knew how precious her diary was to Anne."[65]
>
> —Miep Gies, Otto Frank's secretary.

The eight prisoners were held overnight at Gestapo headquarters and then driven to a local prison called Huis van Bewaring (House of Detention). On August 8, 1944, guards took them to the railway station, where they boarded a train for Westerbork, a village in northeastern Netherlands. Upon arrival they would all be housed at a transit camp also called Westerbork. In his book *The Last Seven Months of Anne Frank*, Dutch author Willy Lindwer describes a transit camp as "a part of the deportation apparatus which funneled Jews to various German concentration camps."[68]

After all that Anne had endured, she had plenty of reasons to be terrified as they boarded the train, but her father later recalled that she did not seem afraid. In fact, after two years of being confined in the annex, never once going outside to breathe fresh air or feel the sun on her face, she seemed to be mesmerized by the scenery. "Anne would not move from the window," said Otto. "Outside it was summer. Meadows, stubble fields, and villages flew by. The telephone wires along the right of way curvetted up and down along the windows. It was like freedom."[69]

"Criminal Jews"

Several days later the train arrived at Westerbork. During registration the Franks and the others who had hidden with them were classified as "criminal Jews." This designation was for those who had been in hiding or tried to escape deportation by other means. One of the ways Jews were punished for this behavior was by not being allowed to stay together in the family barracks. Instead, they were separated, with Otto in the men's block and Edith, Anne, and Margot in the women's.

Another penalty for Jews who had attempted to avoid deportation was the type of work they were assigned. As criminal Jews, they were given the hardest, dirtiest jobs. Edith and the girls, for example, worked on breaking batteries apart, and their twelve-hour day began at 5:00 a.m. Working alongside them was Janny Brandes-Brilleslijper, a nurse from Rotterdam, Netherlands, who was imprisoned for being part of the Dutch resistance movement. She describes how filthy and unhealthy the work was: "We had to chop open the batteries with a

The Nazis routinely packed captured Jews into boxcars and shipped them to one of several concentration camps far behind the front lines. When Anne and her family were in transit to a concentration camp, they rode for three days in a crowded cattle car with little ventilation.

chisel and a hammer and then throw the tar in one basket and the carbon bars, which we had to remove, into another basket; we had to take off the metal caps with a screwdriver, and they went into a third basket. In addition to getting terribly dirty from the work, we all began to cough because it gave off a certain kind of dust."[70]

Yet as bad as the assignment was, there was also a benefit to it. Brandes-Brilleslijper says that while they worked, they were able to visit: "The agreeable part of working on the batteries was that you could talk with each other."[71] The women sat at long tables together and tried to keep their conversations as upbeat and positive as possible.

While at Westerbork, Anne made an impression on those who met her, just as she had in Amsterdam. People viewed her as a young woman who, despite her bleak surroundings and uncertain future, remained optimistic and hopeful. "Anne was particularly friendly and social," says Melissa Müller. "People who knew her in Westerbork said her pale face and big eyes glowed with confidence."[72]

Hell Train

Because Westerbork was a transit camp, few prisoners remained there. One of the regular occurrences was a weekly announcement of who was scheduled to be transferred to a different camp. On Saturday, September 2, 1944, the announcement stated that 1,019 men, women, and children would be boarding a train and leaving Westerbork the next morning. A staff member read the names from a list, and included on it were Otto, Edith, Margot, and Anne Frank. No destination was given. They had no idea they were heading for southwest Poland to the largest of the Nazi death camps, Auschwitz-Birkenau.

At dawn on Sunday, Westerbork guards rounded up everyone who was on the list and escorted them to the railroad tracks. The Franks felt fortunate to be traveling together—but were dismayed to see the train waiting on the tracks. Unlike the passenger train that transported them to Westerbork, this was a freight train. The passengers would ride in sealed cars made for transporting cattle. Müller writes: "There were no windows, only two ridiculously small barred openings for ventilation. There were no seats, only a cold floor with a little straw scattered on it."[73] In one corner of the car were two large buckets: one filled with water for drinking, and the other for the passengers to use as a toilet.

A Gruesome Sight

On April 15, 1945, soldiers from Britain's Eleventh Armoured Division entered the Bergen-Belsen concentration camp to liberate the prisoners—and were horrified at what they found. The US Holocaust Memorial Museum explains: "Inside were more than 60,000 emaciated and ill prisoners in desperate need of medical attention. More than 13,000 corpses in various stages of decomposition lay littered around the camp. . . . Conditions within the grossly overpopulated camp in 1945 were horrendous." Surrounded by death and disease and living in lice-infested squalor, five hundred people were dying each day.

General Hugh Llewellyn Glyn-Hughes, deputy director of the British army's medical services division, was given a formidable assignment: feeding tens of thousands of starving people, curtailing the spread of infectious disease, and burying the dead. Food and water supplies arrived and were distributed without delay. The death rate began to decline, but many prisoners were too weak and sick to survive. Thus, three hundred to four hundred people were still dying each day. Within a month, relief squads had reduced the number of deaths to fewer than one hundred per day. People were transferred out of the former concentration camp to hospitals or other facilities, and the dead were buried in mass graves. The final task was burning down the barracks. On May 21, 1945, the British soldiers burned the last barracks of the camp in a ceremonial burning. Says the US Holocaust Memorial Museum: "Bergen-Belsen became a watchword for Nazi inhumanity and brutality."

US Holocaust Memorial Museum, "The 11th Armoured Division (Great Britain)," June 20, 2014. www.ushmm.org.

At least seventy people were packed into each railcar, "crowded to the point of near suffocation,"[74] says Müller. The fortunate ones found a place in a corner or along the sides so they had something to lean on. One of the passengers later said that Anne had been leaning on her father's shoulder. As soon as the car was stuffed with people, the guards shoved the metal door shut and secured it with a heavy metal bar. "It was pitch black inside," says Müller. "The glimmer of light that came in through the vents was useless. And after a few minutes, the air was so foul that people could hardly breathe."[75]

The Death Camp

The journey lasted for three days and two nights. When the train finally screeched to a halt, the passengers had no idea what day it was or where they were; all sense of time and distance had been lost on the dreadful train ride. The doors of the cattle cars were slammed open, and the disoriented passengers were blinded by glaring searchlights. Nazi guards armed with machine guns were shouting, ordering everyone to move, to move faster, shoving them along if they were dragging behind.

The scene was unimaginable chaos, as Sam Gottesman, who was on the same train as the Franks, explains: "It was an unbelievable sight. There was so much confusion everywhere. People were screaming, frightened children were crying, prisoners with shaven heads and striped uniforms were running around, and SS guards with large police dogs were pushing the people in different directions. I thought I was in a nightmare."[76] Within a day more than five hundred passengers from that train were sent to the gas chambers—including all children under age fifteen. Anne was spared immediate death because her age was fifteen years and three months.

Guards separated the males and females and moved them to different areas. All prisoners had numbers tattooed on their left forearms. The next stage was known as "disinfection." After being ordered to strip naked, each person's hair was shaved off. This included underarm hair, pubic hair, and the hair on their heads. Anne's hair had been a long, lustrous brown, and she had taken great pride in it. "For Anne," says Müller, "her hair had always been an important means of expressing her

> *"For Anne, her hair had always been an important means of expressing her personality. And that was precisely the point for the Nazis: to deprive Jews of their personalities."*[77]
>
> —Melissa Müller, Anne Frank biographer.

48

This modern photo of a barracks at Auschwitz-Birkenau reveals how Jewish prisoners were stacked in cramped quarters. Anne and Margot slept in quarters like these, where every day they suffered plagues of bedbugs and disease.

personality. And that was precisely the point for the Nazis: to deprive Jews of their personalities." Müller goes on to say that the last step of disinfection of the female prisoners was herding the "naked, bald, thirsty, and totally demoralized women"[77] and girls into a large community shower room. Without warning, water suddenly gushed down on them, from scalding hot to icy cold. They were not given towels; naked and dripping wet, they were led out of the showers and given shapeless dresses to wear. They were then assigned to the women's barracks.

Although Anne, Margot, and Edith were relieved they could stay together, the barracks were dreadful. The sleeping cots were infested with fleas, bedbugs, and parasitic mites that caused a contagious skin condition known as scabies. "These parasites bored into their weakened victims," says Müller, "and left itchy bumps that turned into painful abscesses and open wounds if they were scratched with dirty fingers."[78] Anne soon developed a severe case of scabies that covered her entire body. She was quarantined to an infirmary known as the scabies

Comforting a Dying Girl

Little is known about Anne Frank's death; even the date is in question, with original reports saying March 1945 and more recent claims that it was February of that year. What is known, based on the testimonies of people who were with her at Bergen-Belsen, was that Anne was gravely ill with the bacterial disease called typhus. In her weakened state, being starved and dehydrated, she would have been especially vulnerable. But when Anne died, according to Holocaust survivor Irma Sonnenberg Menkel, she did not die alone.

Menkel was transferred to Bergen-Belsen from the Westerbork transit camp. Against her wishes she was chosen to be leader of her barracks, in which five hundred women and girls lived. Among them were Anne, Margot, and Edith Frank. "Conditions were extremely crowded and unsanitary," says Menkel. Disease was rampant at the camp. "Typhus was a terrible problem, especially for children. Of 500 in my barracks, maybe 100 got it and most of them died. Many others starved to death." She got to know Anne and became fond of her: "She was a nice, fine person." When Anne developed typhus, Menkel tried to console her. "She would say to me, 'Irma, I am very sick.' I said, 'No, you are not so sick.' She wanted to be reassured that she wasn't." Finally, Anne's body gave out. "When she slipped into a coma," says Menkel, "I took her in my arms. She didn't know that she was dying. She didn't know that she was so sick. You never know."

Irma Sonnenberg Menkel, "I Saw Anne Frank Die," *Newsweek*, July 20, 1997. www.newsweek.com.

block, where conditions were even worse than in the main camp. Yet Margot would not let her sister go there alone; she went along with her and also caught scabies. Edith was desperate to help her daughters, so she dug a hole under the scabies block and passed them her piece of bread. "As long as she could be near her children," says Müller, "Edith gladly went without food herself."[79]

Edith and her daughters were together at Auschwitz for about eight weeks. Then, at the end of October 1944, Edith was separated from Anne and Margot for the first time. The girls were transported by freight train to a camp in northwestern Germany called Bergen-Belsen. Grief-stricken, malnourished, and thoroughly exhausted, Edith died just over two months after her daughters were taken from her.

Too Weak to Fight

The train carrying Anne and Margot, as well as more than thirteen hundred other women, arrived at Bergen-Belsen a few days later. It had long been known as one of the "nicer" concentration camps. Many Jews who were confined there spoke of the conditions being markedly better than what they had endured at Auschwitz-Birkenau. One of these was a Hungarian Jewish woman named Marika Frank Abrams, who says that when she arrived at Bergen-Belsen, she and the other new arrivals received two blankets and a food dish. "There was running water and latrines," says Abrams. "We were given food that was edible and [we] didn't have to stand for hours to be counted. The conditions were so superior to Auschwitz we felt we were practically at a sanitarium."[80]

By the time Anne and Margot arrived at Bergen-Belsen, the camp had deteriorated badly and conditions were deplorable. This was largely caused by severe overcrowding. Originally designed to hold ten thousand prisoners, the Bergen-Belsen population was nearly double that by December 1944. At the beginning of March 1945, the number of prisoners had grown to forty-two thousand and jumped to fifty thousand one month later. In *The Last Seven Months of Anne Frank*, Lindwer writes: "Living conditions in this camp . . . were so bad that, although there were no gas chambers, ten thousand people died." Lindwer goes on to say that in order to accommodate the burgeoning prison population, numerous barracks had been added. But rather than improve the camp, this only made conditions worse. "There was almost nothing to eat," he says, "it was winter, and sickness and disease were everywhere."[81]

> "Living conditions in [Bergen-Belsen] . . . were so bad that, although there were no gas chambers, ten thousand people died."[81]
>
> —Willy Lindwer, Anne Frank biographer.

One disease that swept through the overcrowded camp was typhus. Caused by fleas, mites, or lice that carry bacteria from infected rats or other rodents, typhus is highly contagious and deadly. Thousands of people at Bergen-Belsen were infected with it, including Margot and Anne. Because they were already so weak from exhaustion and starvation, they became desperately ill. Janny Brandes-Brilleslijper, with whom the Franks had made friends at Westerbork, was at Bergen-Belsen. She was heartbroken at seeing Anne, who was emaciated and sick, a shadow of the bright-eyed, cheerful young woman Brandes-

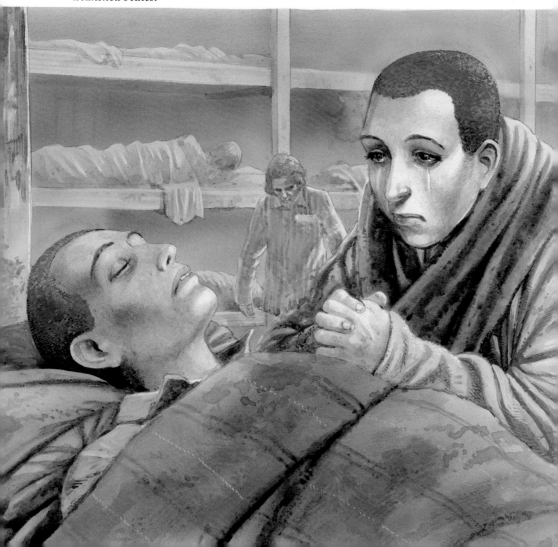

After being moved to the Bergen-Belsen camp in the fall of 1944, Anne and Margot faced cold weather and starvation in overcrowded conditions. Illnesses spread quickly; both Margot and Anne caught typhus, the disease that would claim their weakened bodies.

Brilleslijper had known. She describes Anne's physical condition during the winter of 1945 when she was dying of typhus:

> At a certain moment in the final days, Anne stood in front of me, wrapped in a blanket. She didn't have any more tears. Oh, we hadn't had tears for a long time. And she told me that she had such a horror of the lice and fleas in her clothes and that she had thrown all of her clothes away. It was the middle of winter and she was wrapped in one blanket. I gathered up everything I could find to give her so she was dressed again. We didn't have much to eat . . . but I gave Anne some of our bread ration.[82]

Two days later, Brandes-Brilleslijper went to look for Anne and found that both she and her sister had passed away. Margot, also sick with typhus, had fallen out of bed onto the stone floor, and that was where she died. Shortly afterward, at the age of fifteen, Anne died.

A "Broken Girl"

Before Anne's death, Hanneli Goslar, her childhood friend who was also at Bergen-Belsen, was able to talk to her a few times. Although it was strictly forbidden, they met in the dark and spoke on either side of a tall barbed-wire fence. During one meeting, Anne was weeping and saying that she had no one left: Her parents were dead and her sister was very sick. She had learned that her mother had died at Auschwitz, and she assumed that her father had died there too—but he had not. Referring to Anne as a "broken girl," Goslar wonders if her tragic story might have had a different ending—a much happier one. "I always think," says Goslar, "if Anne had known her father was still alive, she might have had more strength to survive."[83]

"I always think if Anne had known her father was still alive, she might have had more strength to survive."[83]

—Hanneli Goslar, Anne's childhood friend.

Chapter Five

A Young Girl's Words Live On

In late January 1945 Soviet troops liberated Auschwitz-Birkenau and set 7,650 prisoners free. One of those prisoners was Otto Frank. Having been forcibly separated from his wife and daughters for months, he rushed to the women's camp at Auschwitz, hoping to find them. When he was told that Edith had died, he was crushed. But there was some news that gave him hope: It was likely that Anne and Margot had been transferred to Bergen-Belsen. Otto knew it was a work camp, not a death camp, so maybe his girls would be coming home soon.

Heartbreaking News

Otto traveled a long, arduous journey by boat, rail, and truck to get from Auschwitz back home to the Netherlands. Upon arriving in Amsterdam, he went to the home of Miep Gies, who was overjoyed to see him. Otto sadly explained that Edith was gone, but he had high hopes that his daughters were alive. He moved in with Gies and her husband and began his tireless search for Anne and Margot. He wrote numerous letters, pored over lists of survivors as soon as they were posted for the public, and even placed an advertisement in the newspaper. Still, he heard nothing about his daughters.

Finally, a letter arrived on July 18, 1945. According to Gies, Otto was in the main office of the Prinsengracht building at the time. He opened the letter to find that it was from Janny Brandes-Brilleslijper, who explained that she had been with Anne and Margot at Bergen-Belsen. She went on to express her sorrow that they had both died of typhus while at the camp. After reading the letter, in a choked voice,

Otto said to Gies: "Margot and Anne are not coming back."[84] He then went to his office and closed the door.

Gies sat at her desk in shock. She had been certain that the girls had survived, and now she had to accept that they were both gone. She then remembered Anne's papers and books that she had placed in her desk drawer nearly a year before. It had been her intention to give them to Anne, but now that would not be possible. So, Gies decided to give them to Anne's father. She pulled everything out of the drawer, piled it into a neat stack with the red plaid diary on top, and took it into Otto's office. She explains: "I held out the diary and the papers to him. I said, 'Here is your daughter Anne's legacy to you.'"[85]

Discovering a Different Anne

Otto was speechless. Of course he and the others who hid in the annex had known that Anne kept a diary; she seemed to always be scribbling in it in her room and was fiercely protective when anyone asked to see it. But he had no idea her writings had been saved after the Nazis raided the annex. Holding her diary and journals in his hands, Otto felt a mix of emotions. To know that she was gone from him forever was unbearably painful; yet by having her writings, it was as though a part of her lived on. He looked at Gies. "Please see to it that I'm not disturbed,"[86] he said. She quietly closed the door and walked away.

> "[In the diary], there was revealed a completely different Anne to the child that I had lost. I had no idea of the depths of her thoughts and feelings."[87]
>
> —Otto Frank, Anne Frank's father.

At first Otto read slowly, only a few pages each day. "More would have been impossible," he later said, "as I was overwhelmed by painful memories." As he kept reading, he became so engrossed in Anne's chronicle of her life that he found it impossible to put her diary down. "For me, it was a revelation," he said. "There was revealed a completely different Anne to the child that I had lost. I had no idea of the depths of her thoughts and feelings."[87] By reading Anne's diary, Otto learned how deeply she was affected by Jewish suffering and also how her faith in God helped keep her strong.

Anne Frank: Birth, Life, and Death

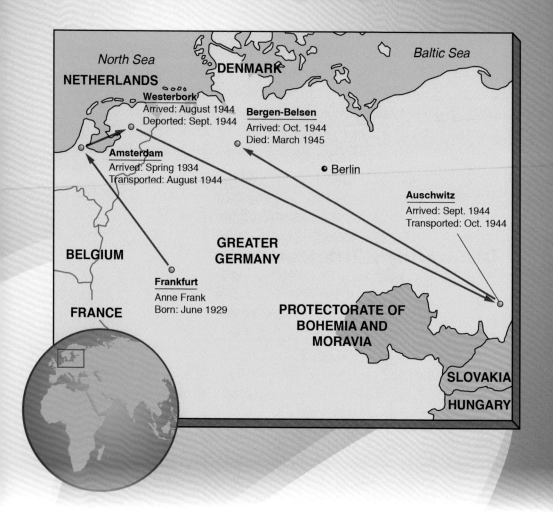

North Sea

NETHERLANDS

DENMARK

Baltic Sea

Westerbork
Arrived: August 1944
Deported: Sept. 1944

Bergen-Belsen
Arrived: Oct. 1944
Died: March 1945

Amsterdam
Arrived: Spring 1934
Transported: August 1944

● Berlin

Auschwitz
Arrived: Sept. 1944
Transported: Oct. 1944

BELGIUM

GREATER GERMANY

Frankfurt
Anne Frank
Born: June 1929

PROTECTORATE OF BOHEMIA AND MORAVIA

FRANCE

SLOVAKIA

HUNGARY

As he continued to read, Otto was taken aback by Anne's fascination with nature, since he could not remember that being a passion of hers. "How could I have known how much it meant for her to see a patch of blue sky, to observe the flying seagulls, or how important that chestnut tree was to her, when she had never shown an interest in nature before," he said. But then it made sense to him: When nature was out of her reach, she began to yearn for it. "Once she felt like a caged bird, how she longed for it," he said. "Even just the thought of the open air gave her comfort, but she kept all these feelings to herself."[88]

One of the dreams Anne had written about was her desire to some-day become a writer. In her diary entry of May 11, 1944, she expressed that it was her "greatest wish" to become a journalist. Once she had succeeded at that, she wanted to become a "famous" writer. "Whether these leanings towards greatness (or insanity?) will ever materialize remains to be seen," Anne wrote, "but I certainly have the subjects in my mind." She described the book that she intended to write. It would be called *Het Achterhuis*, which is Dutch for "The Annex" (or "The Back House"). She explained: "Whether I shall succeed or not, I cannot say, but my diary will be a great help. I have other ideas as well besides *Het Achterhuis*. But I will write more fully about them some other time, when they have taken a clearer form in my mind."[89]

Bringing Anne's Dream to Life

Because Anne's goal of becoming a writer and having *Het Achterhuis* published were clearly spelled out in her diary, there was no doubt what her plans were. So Otto intended to carry them out for her. He read through the diary and notebooks, as well as the loose sheets of paper. He then compiled it all into a typewritten manuscript. This took several rounds of revisions; although Otto had no way of knowing exactly what Anne wanted, he did his best to do what he thought she would want. He read through the manuscript multiple times, made editing changes, and then asked several friends to read it and give their opinions and suggestions. These friends included journalist Jan Romein, a playwright named Albert Cauvern, and Kurt Baschwitz, a German journalist and Holocaust survivor. All three had positive remarks about the manuscript, with Baschwitz showering it with praise. In a letter, he wrote that *Het Achterhuis* was "the most moving document about that time that I know" and called it "a literary masterpiece."[90]

Otto was driven to see his daughter's work published. By having her diary in print, he would be helping Anne realize her dream of becoming a writer, even though it would happen posthumously. "He carried the manuscript wherever he went," says Francine Prose, "and, at times, tears flowed down his face as he read a few pages aloud, or urged friends and strangers to read it." Prose goes on to say that "the edited typescript was passed from hand to hand and across desks," but still, every editor who read the manuscript rejected it. Not one of them, says Prose, "could imagine that readers would buy the intimate diary of a teenage girl, dead in the war. In addition, the Dutch had no desire to be reminded of the suffering they had so recently endured."[91]

Romein, one of the manuscript's most avid supporters, adamantly disagreed with that perception. On April 3, 1946, he wrote about the diary in the daily newspaper *Het Parool*, which had formerly been the underground paper of the Dutch resistance movement. In the article, which was titled "Children's Voice," Romein praised Anne's work. He said it was a more powerful indictment against fascism than any evidence that had thus far been presented. Romein ended by describing the profound effect Anne's writings had on him personally. "When I had finished it was nighttime, and I was astonished to find that the lights still worked, and we still had bread and tea, that I could hear no airplanes droning overhead and no pounding of army boots in the street—I had been engrossed in my reading, so carried away back to that unreal world, now almost a year behind us."[92]

> *"The English reading public would avert their eyes from so painful a story which would bring back to them all the evil events that occurred during the war."*[95]
>
> —A publishing house editor from London, England.

After Romein's article appeared on the front page of *Het Parool*, several publishers contacted Otto Frank. Otto chose to work with Contact, a publishing house based in Amsterdam. After cutting some material from the diary that was deemed inappropriate by editors, Contact printed *Het Achterhuis* and released it in the Netherlands in 1947. The book was fairly successful and was reprinted again several times. Along the way its title was changed to *The Diary of a Young Girl*.

When the first edition of *Diary* was released, Otto noted the momentous date in his appointment book with the word *Boek*, meaning "book." Later he reflected on that day, saying: "If she had been here, Anne would have been so proud."[93]

Snubbed

Unfortunately, the reception was not so positive in the United States. According to Prose, it was rejected by nearly every major publishing house. A friend of Otto's who lived in New York City, Ernst Kuhn, took it upon himself to find a US publisher for Anne's book. He soon learned, however, that doing so was a formidable task. He was told, over and over again, that Americans were not interested in reading books about the war. An editor from New York's Vanguard Press said to Kuhn: "Under

Anne's Dream Comes to the Stage

On October 5, 1955, a play called *The Diary of Anne Frank* premiered on Broadway at New York City's Cort Theatre. The script was written by the husband-and-wife playwright team of Albert Hackett and Frances Goodrich. Otto Frank had read and approved the script, believing that even though it was not exactly like Anne's book, it captured the essence of it. He also met with the actors and helped them prepare for their roles. He would not, however, attend the play, and he explained why in a letter to everyone involved in the production: "This play is a part of my life, and the idea that my wife and children as well as I will be presented on the stage is a painful one to me. Therefore it is impossible for me to come and see it."

The Diary of Anne Frank was critically acclaimed and highly praised by the public. The play also received prestigious awards such as the esteemed Pulitzer Prize for Drama, the Tony Award for Best Play, and the New York Drama Critics' Circle Award for Best Play. In November 1956 the play premiered in the Netherlands, with Queen Juliana and Prince Bernhard in attendance. When it was presented in Germany, more than 2 million people attended.

Quoted in Anne Frank House, "A Play and on Film." www.annefrank.org.

the present frame of mind of the American public, you cannot publish a book with war as a background."[94] Other publishers, such as Knopf, rejected the manuscript because Americans were not familiar with the people featured in it. Viking was not interested in publishing it either.

The British reaction was much the same. A prominent London publishing house called Secker and Warburg said that the book would not sell in Britain. Memories of living during the war were still too fresh in people's minds for them to want to read about it. An editor wrote: "The English reading public would avert their eyes from so painful a story which would bring back to them all the evil events that occurred during the war."[95]

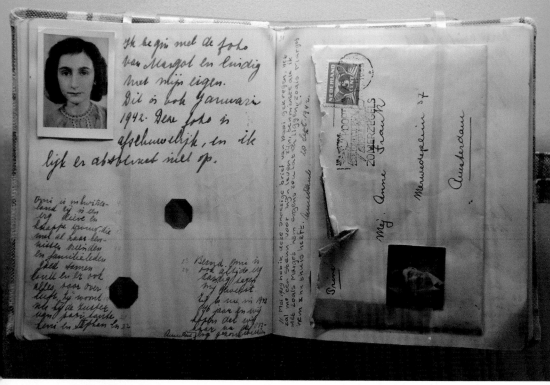

In the pages of one of her diaries, Anne Frank expressed her desire to survive the war and become a famous writer. Although she perished in the camps, Anne's written descriptions of her experiences growing up and the specifics of her tragedy have made her very well known.

The Diary of a Young Girl

A young American editorial assistant had a very different viewpoint— she was convinced that Anne's book would not only sell, it would captivate readers. Judith Jones worked for Doubleday at the time, in its Paris, France, office. One day while her boss, Frank Price, was at lunch, Jones found the French edition of *The Diary of a Young Girl* in his reject pile. She took it out of the pile and started reading it, and she found it so riveting she could not put it down. She explains:

> All afternoon, I remained curled up on the sofa, sharing Anne's life in the attic, until the last light was gone and I heard Frank's key at the front door. Surprised to find me still there, he was even more surprised to hear that it was Anne Frank who had kept me. But he was finally persuaded by my enthusiasm and let me get the book off to Doubleday in New York, urging them to publish it.[96]

Jones (who later became a top editor at Knopf) goes on to say that it did not take much urging at all. Doubleday offered Otto Frank a contract, and *The Diary of a Young Girl* was published in the United States. Although initial sales were modest, the book's popularity continued to grow. Over time it became one of the most celebrated and famous chronicles of the Holocaust ever written.

According to the Anne Frank Center USA, since its first publication in 1947, Anne Frank's diary has been translated into sixty-seven languages with more than 30 million copies sold. The center writes:

Unfounded Accusations

In the years since Anne Frank's *Diary of a Young Girl* was published, a number of people have alleged that the diary was a forgery. Up until his death in 1980, Otto Frank fought these false allegations in court. In 1979, when Otto was ninety years old, he commented on the unfortunate situation: "At the moment there are four court cases in West Germany, two in Hamburg and two in Frankfurt, concerning accusations that the diary is a forgery. I fought against this in 1961 and won, but the same accusations are still being expressed, and I have to fight against them over and over again." After Otto's death his benefactors, the Anne Frank House and the Anne Frank Fonds charitable foundation, assumed responsibility for defending Anne's legacy.

One of those who made false accusations was a German man named Heinz Roth. Through his publishing company, Roth distributed pro-Nazi pamphlets with titles such as "The Diary of Anne Frank—a Forgery" and "The Diary of Anne Frank—the Great Fraud." Otto Frank filed suit against Roth in 1976 before the District Court in Frankfurt. Two years later the court ruled in Otto's favor, stating that Roth must not make those or any similar statements in public or he would be forced to pay substantial fines. Roth appealed and in 1979 his appeal was rejected.

Quoted in Anne Frank House, "Otto Reconciles." www.annefrank.org.

"Its message of courage and hope in the face of adversity has reached millions.... Anne Frank's story is especially meaningful to young people today. For many she is their first, if not their only, exposure to the history of the Holocaust."[97]

"A Legacy to the World"

Gies died in January 2010, just one month short of her 101st birthday. In her book *Anne Frank Remembered*, she spoke freely about her hesitation to read Anne's book. From the day she gave the diary and journals to Otto up until it was published, she would not read it. Even when he

Miep Gies, Otto Frank's secretary, stands by a photo of Anne that was displayed at the 1995 publication of the definitive edition of Anne Frank: The Diary of a Young Girl. *Gies helped hide the Franks, and she was the person who saved Anne's diaries for posterity.*

wanted to read passages out loud to her, she refused. "I could not bring myself to listen," she said. "It was much too upsetting to me."[98] Finally, Gies agreed to read it in 1947. Like so many people since that time, once she started reading she could not stop. "From the first word, I heard Anne's voice come back to speak to me from where she had gone," Gies said. "I lost track of time. Anne's voice tumbled out of the book, so full of life, moods, curiosity, feelings. She was no longer gone and destroyed. She was alive again in my mind."[99]

> "Anne Frank's story is especially meaningful to young people today. For many she is their first, if not their only, exposure to the history of the Holocaust."[97]
>
> —Anne Frank Center USA.

After finishing the diary, Gies did not feel the sadness and grief she had expected. As she explained in her book about Anne: "When I had read the last word, I didn't feel the pain I'd anticipated. I was glad I'd read it at last. The emptiness in my heart was eased. So much had been lost, but now Anne's voice would never be lost. My young friend had left a remarkable legacy to the world."[100]

Source Notes

Introduction: Holding On to Hope

1. Doris L. Bergen, *The Holocaust: A Concise History*. Lanham, MD: Rowman & Littlefield, 2009, p. viii.

2. Anne Frank, *The Diary of a Young Girl*, New York: Doubleday, 1967, p. ix.

3. Frank, *The Diary of a Young Girl*, p. 4.

4. Frank, *The Diary of a Young Girl*, p. 5.

Chapter 1: Early Childhood in Germany

5. Melissa Müller, *Anne Frank*. New York: Metropolitan, 1998, p. 19.

6. Müller, *Anne Frank*, p. 22.

7. Ronald Wilfred Jansen, *Anne Frank: Silent Witnesses*. Drenthe, Netherlands: RWJ, 2014, p. 22.

8. Francine Prose, *Anne Frank: The Book, the Life, the Afterlife*. New York: Harper Perennial, 2010, p. 25.

9. Jansen, *Anne Frank*, p. 25.

10. Müller, *Anne Frank*, p. 16.

11. US Holocaust Memorial Museum, "World War I: Treaties and Reparations," June 20, 2014. www.ushmm.org.

12. Müller, *Anne Frank*, p. 20.

13. London Jewish Cultural Centre, "The Immediate Effects of the Wall Street Crash," Holocaust Explained, 2011. www.theholo caustexplained.org.

14. Müller, *Anne Frank*, p. 21.

15. Anti-Defamation League, "Overview of the Holocaust: 1933–1945," 2012. www.adl.org.

16. US Holocaust Memorial Museum, "Hitler Comes to Power." www.ushmm.org.

17. US Holocaust Memorial Museum, "Hitler Comes to Power."

18. Quoted in Anne Frank House, "Life in Germany." www.annefrank.org.

19. Quoted in Müller, *Anne Frank*, p. 27.

20. Bergen, *The Holocaust*, p. 58.

21. Quoted in Anne Frank House, "Emigration Plans." www.annefrank.org.

Chapter 2: Evil Closes In

22. Müller, *Anne Frank*, p. 52.

23. Quoted in Aviva Loeb, "Anne Frank's Childhood Friend: We Have to Try to Live in Peace Together," *Jerusalem Post*, July 22, 2014. www.jpost.com.

24. Müller, *Anne Frank*, p. 53.

25. Miep Gies with Alison Leslie Gold, *Anne Frank Remembered*. New York: Glencoe/McGraw-Hill, 2002, p. 31.

26. Müller, *Anne Frank*, p. 55.

27. Quoted in *Mirror Online*, "My Friend Anne Frank: Classmate on the Girl Behind the World's Most Famous Diary," January 3, 2009. www.mirror.co.uk.

28. Gies, *Anne Frank Remembered*, p. 33.

29. Müller, *Anne Frank*, p. 64.

30. Gies, *Anne Frank Remembered*, p. 26.

31. Linda M. Woolf, "Survival and Resistance: The Netherlands Under Nazi Occupation," Webster University, April 6, 1999. www2.webster.edu.

32. Gies, *Anne Frank Remembered*, p. 37.

33. Prose, *Anne Frank*, p. 34.

34. Frank, *The Diary of a Young Girl*, p. 4.

35. Müller, *Anne Frank*, p. 136.

36. Frank, *The Diary of a Young Girl*, p. 5.

37. Müller, *Anne Frank*, pp. 145–46.

38. Frank, *The Diary of a Young Girl*, p. 14.

39. Anne Frank, *The Diary of a Young Girl: The Definitive Edition*. New York: Doubleday, 1995. http://blog.shahariaazam.com.

Chapter 3: A Secret Existence

40. Frank, *The Diary of a Young Girl*, p. 17.

41. Frank, *The Diary of a Young Girl*, p. 17.

42. Frank, *The Diary of a Young Girl*, p. 18.

43. Frank, *The Diary of a Young Girl*, p. 20.

44. Frank, *The Diary of a Young Girl*, p. 20.

45. Frank, *The Diary of a Young Girl*, p. 20.

46. Frank, *The Diary of a Young Girl*, p. 22.

47. Frank, *The Diary of a Young Girl*, p. 22.

48. Frank, *The Diary of a Young Girl*, p. 24.

49. Gies, *Anne Frank Remembered*, p. 74.

50. Gies, *Anne Frank Remembered*, p. 75.

51. Müller, *Anne Frank*, p. 168.

52. Gies, *Anne Frank Remembered*, p. 72.

53. Frank, *The Diary of a Young Girl*, p. 110.

54. Frank, *The Diary of a Young Girl*, p. 111.

55. Gies, *Anne Frank Remembered*, p. 89.

56. Gies, *Anne Frank Remembered*, p. 89.

57. Frank, *The Diary of a Young Girl*, pp. 59–60.

58. Frank, *The Diary of a Young Girl*, pp. 60–61.

59. Frank, *The Diary of a Young Girl*, p. 122.

60. Frank, *The Diary of a Young Girl*, p. 35.

61. Frank, *The Diary of a Young Girl*, p. 72.

62. Frank, *The Diary of a Young Girl*, p. 270.

63. Gies, *Anne Frank Remembered*, p. 139.

64. Quoted in Gies, *Anne Frank Remembered*, p. 139.

Chapter 4: The Beginning of the End

65. Gies, *Anne Frank Remembered*, p. 143.

66. Gies, *Anne Frank Remembered*, p. 144.

67. Prose, *Anne Frank*, p. 53.

68. Willy Lindwer, *The Last Seven Months of Anne Frank*. New York: Anchor Books, 1992, p. 4.

69. Quoted in Anne Frank House, "To Camp Westerbork." www.anne frank.org.

70. Quoted in Lindwer, *The Last Seven Months of Anne Frank*, p. 6

71. Quoted in Lindwer, *The Last Seven Months of Anne Frank*, p. 6.

72. Müller, *Anne Frank*, p. 236.

73. Müller, *Anne Frank*, p. 242.

74. Müller, *Anne Frank*, p. 242.

75. Müller, *Anne Frank*, p. 242.

76. Quoted in Betty Merti, *The World of Anne Frank: A Complete Resource Guide*. Portland, ME: Walch, 1998, p. 29.

77. Müller, *Anne Frank*, p. 248.

78. Müller, *Anne Frank*, p. 248.

79. Müller, *Anne Frank*, p. 251.

80. Quoted in Mark Weber, "Bergen-Belsen Camp: The Suppressed Story," *Journal of Historical Review*, May/June 1995. www.ihr.org.

81. Lindwer, *The Last Seven Months of Anne Frank*.

82. Quoted in Lindwer, *The Last Seven Months of Anne Frank*.

83. Quoted in Prose, *Anne Frank*, p. 57.

Chapter 5: A Young Girl's Words Live On

84. Quoted in Gies, *Anne Frank Remembered*, p. 170.

85. Gies, *Anne Frank Remembered*, p. 171.

86. Quoted in Gies, *Anne Frank Remembered*, p. 171.

87. Quoted in Anne Frank House, "Otto Reads Anne's Diary." www.annefrank.org.

88. Quoted in Anne Frank House, "Otto Reads Anne's Diary."

89. Frank, *The Diary of a Young Girl*, p. 260.

90. Quoted in Prose, *Anne Frank*, p. 77.

91. Prose, *Anne Frank*, p. 77.

92. Quoted in Prose, *Anne Frank*, p. 78.

93. Quoted in Anne Frank House, "Anne Frank's Diary Is Published." www.annefrank.org.

94. Quoted in Prose, *Anne Frank*, p. 81.

95. Quoted in Prose, *Anne Frank*, p. 81.

96. Quoted in Prose, *Anne Frank*, p. 82.

97. Anne Frank Center USA, "About Anne Frank," 2015. http://annefrank.com.

98. Gies, *Anne Frank Remembered*, p. 175.

99. Gies, *Anne Frank Remembered*, p. 180.

100. Gies, *Anne Frank Remembered*, p. 180.

Important Events in the Life of Anne Frank

1929

Anne Frank is born in Frankfurt, Germany, to Edith Holländer Frank and Otto Frank.

1930

Economic damage from the 1929 collapse of the New York Stock Exchange spreads throughout the world, hitting the German economy especially hard. The German people grow increasingly upset with government.

1932

The Nazi Party, once a small splinter group with few followers, wins the majority of seats in the German parliament.

1933

Nazi leader Adolf Hitler is appointed chancellor of Germany; later that year the Franks leave Germany and immigrate to Amsterdam, Holland, in the Netherlands.

1934

Anne starts kindergarten in the Montessori school in Amsterdam.

1938

Germany annexes neighboring Austria, forming a new German province called Ostmark.

1939

Germany invades Poland and Czechoslovakia. In August Hitler issues a statement vowing to respect the Netherlands' neutrality.

1940

Germany invades Denmark and Norway; a month later the Germans also invade the Netherlands.

1941

In keeping with new anti-Jewish laws in the Netherlands, Anne and Margot leave their present school and attend a school for Jews only.

1942

For her thirteenth birthday, Anne receives a treasured gift: a diary with a red, tan, and light green plaid cover; the following month Anne and her family leave their home and go into hiding to escape the growing dangers to Jews posed by Nazis.

1944

An unknown betrayer notifies police about the Jews living in the attic space; all are arrested and taken away to Gestapo headquarters. Edith and Otto end up at Auschwitz-Birkenau in Poland; Anne and Margot ultimately end up at Bergen-Belsen concentration camp in Germany.

1945

In February or March Anne and Margo die of typhus at Bergen-Belsen. In April the camp is liberated and Germany surrenders, thereby ending the war in Europe. In October Otto receives a letter saying that both his daughters died at Bergen-Belsen.

1947

Fifteen hundred copies of Anne's diary are published by Contact Publishers in Amsterdam.

1950

Anne's diary is published in Germany and France.

1952

Anne's diary is translated into English and published in the United States.

1955

A play titled *The Diary of Anne Frank* opens on Broadway. One year later it wins the Tony Award for Best Play and the Pulitzer Prize for Drama.

For Further Research

Books

Anne Frank, *The Diary of a Young Girl: The Definitive Edition*. New York: Penguin Random House, 2010.

Miep Gies with Alison Leslie Gold, *Anne Frank Remembered*. New York: Simon & Schuster, 2009.

Ronald Wilfred Jansen, *Anne Frank: Silent Witnesses*. Drenthe, Netherlands: RWJ, 2014.

Melissa Müller, *Anne Frank*. New York: Metropolitan, 2013.

Francine Prose, *Anne Frank: The Book, the Life, the Afterlife*. New York: Harper Perennial, 2010.

Internet Sources

Anti-Defamation League, "Overview of the Holocaust: 1933–1945," 2012. www.adl.org/assets/pdf/education-outreach/Overview-of-the-Holocaust-NYLM-Guide.pdf.

Justin Huggler, "Friend Tells of Tragic Last Meeting with Anne Frank," *Telegraph*, March 9, 2015. www.telegraph.co.uk.

Madison Park, "Researchers Say Anne Frank Perished Earlier than Thought," CNN, April 5, 2015. www.cnn.com/2015/04/01/europe/anne-frank-date-of-death.

MSN, Anne Frank's Life in Photos: 70 Years Since Her Death," March 6, 2015. www.msn.com/en-us/news/photos/anne-franks-life-in-photos-70-years-since-her-death/ss-BBibRI9.

Stan Ziv, "From Pseudonym to Speaking Out: Anne Frank's Best Friend," *Newsweek*, June 28, 2015. www.newsweek.com/pseudonym-speaking-out-conversation-anne-franks-best-friend-347960.

Websites

Anne Frank Fonds (www.annefrank.ch). Established as a charitable foundation in 1963 by Otto Frank, Anne Frank Fonds holds the rights for the works, letters, and photos of Anne Frank and her family members. A wealth of information about Anne Frank and her family can be found on the site.

Anne Frank House (www.annefrank.org). Anne Frank House oversees the Anne Frank House museum in Amsterdam and works to educate the public about Anne Frank's life. Along with a vast amount of information about Anne Frank, this site features an extensive time line and an interactive "Secret Annex Online."

Holocaust Explained (www.theholocaustexplained.org). Administered by the London Jewish Cultural Centre, this site seeks to teach young people about the Holocaust and help combat anti-Semitism and racism. The website, which is designed for students aged eleven to sixteen, offers valuable lessons about the Holocaust.

US Holocaust Memorial Museum (www.ushmm.org). The USHMM is dedicated to the documentation, study, and interpretation of Holocaust history and serves as a memorial to the millions of people who died during the Holocaust. The website is packed with informational resources.

Index

Note: Boldface page numbers indicate illustrations.

Abrams, Marika Frank, 51
Amsterdam
  Anne's early life in, 21–24
  erosion of rights of Jews in, 27–30
  Frank family moves to, 20
Anne Frank Center USA, 61, 62
Anne Frank: Silent Witnesses (Jansen), 10–11
Anti-Defamation League, 16
anti-Semitism, Hitler's use of, 16
Auschwitz-Birkenau (death camp), 46, **49**, 51
  journey to, 46–48

Baschwitz, Kurt, 57
Bergen, Doris L., 6, 14
Bergen-Belsen (concentration camp), 9, 50, 51–52
  liberation of, 47
book burnings, 14
Brandes-Brilleslijper, Janny, 45–46, 52–53, 54

Cauvern, Albert, 57

Deetman, Julius, 36
Diary of Anne Frank, The (Hackett and Goodrich), 59
Diary of a Young Girl, The (Frank), publication of, 57–61

Enabling Act (1933), 18–19

Frank, Alice Betty Stern (grandmother), 12
Frank, Anne, **8**, **19**
  birth/early childhood of, 10, 13
  death of, 50, 53
  on desire to become a journalist, 56–57
  discovery of diary of, 43
  family background of, 11–12
  on frustrations of life in annex, 39
  life in Amsterdam, 21–24
  on life in the annex, 33–34
Frank, Edith Holländer (mother), 7, 12, 50
  death of, 51

Frank, Margot (sister), 7, 9, **19**, 52, 54
  death of, 53
  receives call-up letter, 30–31
Frank, Michael (grandfather), 11
Frank, Otto (father), 7, 11, 44
  discovers fate of his family, 54–55
  on leaving Germany, 20
  publication of *The Diary* and, 57–58
Frankfurt, Germany, 10–11
Friedländer, Saul, 6

Germany
  anti-Jewish violence grows in, 25–26
  Jewish population of, 16
  rise of Nazi Party in, 15–16
  Treaty of Versailles and, 13–15
Gies, Miep, 22, 24, 36–37, 62, **62**
  on Anne's maturity, 29
  on anti-Jewish uprisings in Amsterdam, 35
  discovery of Anne's diary by, 43, 44
  on discovery of the Franks, 41–42
  efforts of, to save the Franks, 40

in German invasion of Holland, 26
learns of deaths of Anne and Margot, 54–55
on reading *The Diary*, 62
Glyn-Hughes, Hugh Llewellyn, 47
Goebbels, Joseph, 14
Goodrich, Frances, 59
Goslar, Hanneli, 21–22, 24, 53
Gottesman, Sam, 48

Hackett, Albert, 59
Hitler, Adolf, 6, **17**, 18–19, 26
  rise of, 16
Holländer, Abraham, 12
Holocaust, 6

Jansen, Ronald Wilfred, 11, 12
Jews
  forced to wear Star of David patch, 27–28
  Hitler launches boycott of, 18
  Nuremberg laws targeting, 25
  uprisings against, 25–26, 35
Jones, Judith, 60–61

Kleiman, Johannes, 30

Kristallnacht (1938), 26
Kugler, Victor, 30, 42
Kuhn, Ernst, 58

Last Seven Months of Anne Frank, The (Lindwer), 44, 51
Law for the Protection of German Blood and German Honor (1935), 25
Lindwer, Willy, 44, 51
London Jewish Cultural Centre, 15

Maaren, Willem G. van, 36
Mein Kampf (Hitler), 17
Menkel, Irma Sonnenberg, 50
Müller, Melissa, 10, 11, 22, 23
  on anxiety among Jews in Amsterdam, 29–30
  on conditions in Auschwitz, 49–50
  on daily life in annex, 35
  on Franks' life in Germany, 13, 15
  on Star of David patch, 28
  on train trip to Auschwitz, 46–48

Nazis (National Socialist German Workers' Party)
  pageantry and, 14
  rise of, 15–16
Netherlands
  Franks move to, 19–20
  German invasion of, 26–27
  under Nazi control, 27–28
Nuremberg Race Laws (1935), 25

Pels, Auguste van, 9, 33, 35, 39, 44
Pels, Hermann van, 9, 33, 35, 44
Pels, Peter van, 9, 33, 35, 44
Pfeffer, Fritz, 9, 37–38
pogroms (anti-Jewish uprisings), 25–26
  in Amsterdam, 35
Prinsengracht building. *See* secret annex
Prose, Francine, 27, 44
  on efforts to publish *The Diary*, 57, 58
  on Otto Frank, 11, 12
  on suspected betrayer of the Franks, 36

Reich Citizenship Law (1935), 25
Romein, Jan, 57, 58
Roth, Heinz, 61

secret annex, **31**
  Anne's description of, 32–33

choice of, 30
daily life in, 35–37
discovery of, 41–42
the Franks escape to, 32
more fugitives move into,
  35, 37–38
Star of David patch, 27–28,
  28
stock market crash (1929),
  15

Treaty of Versailles (1919),
  14

US Holocaust Memorial
  Museum, 16, 18, 25, 47

Versailles, Treaty of (1919),
  14
Voskuijl, Bep, 30, 43

Westerbork (transit camp),
  44–45, 46
Westerkerk Church, 33, **34**
Woolf, Linda M., 26
World War I, Germany in
  aftermath of, 13–15

Picture Credits

About the Author

Peggy J. Parks holds a bachelor of science degree from Aquinas College in Grand Rapids, Michigan, where she graduated magna cum laude. An author who has written dozens of educational books on a wide variety of topics for children and young adults, Parks lives in Muskegon, Michigan, a town that she says inspires her writing because of its location on the shores of Lake Michigan.